ITIL®

CW00428309

perational Support and Analysis
IL® Intermediate Capability Handbook

itSMF International
The IT Service Management Forum

London: TSO

i

information & publishing solutions

Published by TSO (The Stationery Office)
and available from:

Online
www.tsoshop.co.uk
Mail, Telephone, Fax & E-mail
TSO
PO Box 29, Norwich, NR3 1GN
Telephone orders/General enquiries:
0870 600 5522
Fax orders: 0870 600 5533
E-mail: customer.services@tso.co.uk
Textphone: 0870 240 3701
TSO@Blackwell and other Accredited Agents

The AXELOS logo is a trade mark of
AXELOS Limited

The AXELOS swirl logo is a trade mark of
AXELOS Limited

ITIL® is a registered trade mark of
AXELOS Limited

MSP® is a registered trade mark of
AXELOS Limited

P3O® is a registered trade mark of
AXELOS Limited

PRINCE2® is a registered trade mark of
AXELOS Limited

M_o_R® is a registered trade mark of
AXELOS Limited

The Best Management Practice Portfolio Product
logo is a trade mark of AXELOS Limited

A CIP catalogue record for this book is available
from the British Library

A Library of Congress CIP catalogue record has
been applied for

First edition 2009
Second edition 2013
First published 2013
Second impression 2014

ISBN 9780113314294 Single copy ISBN
ISBN 9780113314300 (Sold in a pack of 10 copies)

Printed in the United Kingdom for The
Stationery Office

Material is FSC certified and produced using
ECF pulp, sourced from fully sustainable forests

P002591037 10/13

Contents

Acknowledgements

SECOND EDITION

Author
Alison Cartlidge, Steria

Reviewers
Oghale Efue, Epsom & Ewell Borough Council
Trevor Murray, The Grey Matters
Sue Shaw, Tricentrica, UK
Paul Wigzel, Paul Wigzel Training & Consultancy

Series editor
Alison Cartlidge, Steria

FIRST EDITION

Authors
Alison Cartlidge, Steria
Janaki Chakravarthy, Infosys
Colin Rudd, itEMS Ltd
John A Sowerby, DHL IT Services

Reviewers

John Groom, West Groom Consulting, UK

Ashley Hanna, HP, UK

Dave Jones, Pink Elephant, UK

Aidan Lawes, service management evangelist, UK

Tricia Lewin, independent consultant, UK

Trevor Murray, The Grey Matters, UK

Michael Imhoff Nielsen, IBM Denmark

Michael Nyhuis, Solisma, Australia

Sue Shaw, Tricentrica, UK

HP Suen, The Hong Kong Jockey Club

Editors

Alison Cartlidge, Steria

Mark Lillycrop, *it*SMF UK

About this guide

This guide provides a quick reference to the processes covered by the ITIL® operational support and analysis (OSA) syllabus. It is designed to act as a study aid for students taking the ITIL Capability qualification for OSA, and as a handy portable reference source for practitioners who work with these processes.

This guide is not intended to replace the more detailed ITIL publications (Cabinet Office, 2011), nor to be a substitute for a course provider's training materials. Many parts of the syllabus require candidates to achieve competence at Bloom Levels 3 and 4, showing the ability to apply their learning and analyse a situation. This study aid focuses on the core knowledge that candidates need to acquire at Bloom Levels 1 and 2, including a knowledge and comprehension of the material that supports the syllabus.

Further syllabus details can be found at:

www.itil-officialsite.com/Qualifications/ITILQualificationScheme.aspx

Listed below in alphabetical order are the ITIL service management processes with cross-references to the publication in which they are primarily defined, and where significant further expansion is provided. Most processes play a role during each lifecycle stage, but only significant references are included. Those processes and functions specifically relevant to the OSA syllabus and covered in this guide are also listed.

ITIL service management processes

Service management process	OSA syllabus	Primary source	Further expansion
Access management	✔	SO	
Availability management		SD	CSI
Business relationship management		SS	SD, CSI
Capacity management		SD	SO, CSI
Change evaluation		ST	
Change management		ST	
Demand management		SS	SD
Design coordination		SD	
Event management	✔	SO	
Financial management for IT services		SS	
Incident management	✔	SO	CSI
Information security management		SD	SO
IT service continuity management		SD	
Knowledge management		ST	CSI
Problem management	✔	SO	
Release and deployment management		ST	
Request fulfilment	✔	SO	

Table continues

Table continued

Service management process	OSA syllabus	Primary source	Further expansion
Service asset and configuration management		ST	
Service catalogue management		SD	SS
Service level management		SD	SS, CSI
Service portfolio management		SS	SD
Service validation and testing		ST	
Seven-step improvement process		CSI	
Strategy management for IT services		SS	
Supplier management		SD	
Transition planning and support		ST	
Function			
Application management	✔	SO	
IT operations management	✔	SO	
Service desk	✔	SO	
Technical management	✔	SO	
SS *ITIL Service Strategy*; SD *ITIL Service Design*; ST *ITIL Service Transition*; SO *ITIL Service Operation*; CSI *ITIL Continual Service Improvement*			

1 Introduction to service management

Note that cross-references in the headings are to section numbers in the ITIL core publications, where more detail can be found. The abbreviations used are: SS *ITIL Service Strategy*; SD *ITIL Service Design*; ST *ITIL Service Transition*; SO *ITIL Service Operation*; and CSI *ITIL Continual Service Improvement*. The core publications are listed in the 'Further guidance and contact points' section at the end.

1.1 BEST PRACTICE (SO 2.1.7)

Organizations operating in dynamic environments need to improve their performance and maintain competitive advantage. Adopting best practices in industry-wide use can help to improve capability.

There are several sources for best practice:

- **Public frameworks and standards** These have been validated across diverse environments; knowledge is widely distributed among professionals; there is publicly available training and certification; acquisition of knowledge through the labour market is easier, as is collaboration and coordination across organizations
- **Proprietary knowledge of organizations and individuals** This is customized for the local context and specific business needs. It may only be available under commercial terms; it may also be tacit knowledge (i.e. inextricable and poorly documented).

1.2   THE ITIL FRAMEWORK (SO 1.2, 1.4)

The ITIL framework is a source of best practice in service management. It is:

- Vendor-neutral
- Non-prescriptive
- Best practice.

ITIL is successful because it describes practices that enable organizations to deliver benefits, return on investment and sustained success. This means that organizations can:

- Deliver value for customers through services, improving customer relationships
- Integrate the strategy for services with the business strategy and customer needs
- Measure, monitor and optimize IT services and service provider performance, and reduce costs
- Manage the IT investment and budget, risks, knowledge, capabilities and resources to deliver services effectively and efficiently
- Enable adoption of a standard approach to service management across the enterprise
- Change the organizational culture to support the achievement of sustained success.

ITIL guidance can be found in the following sets of publications:

- **ITIL core** Best-practice publications applicable to all types of organizations that provide services to a business
- **ITIL complementary guidance** A set of publications with guidance specific to industry sectors, organization types, operating models and technology architectures.

ITIL guidance can be adapted to support various business environments and organizational strategies. Complementary ITIL publications provide flexibility to implement the core in a diverse range of environments.

ITIL has been deployed successfully around the world for more than 20 years. Over this time, the framework has evolved from a specialized set of service management topics with a focus on function, to a process-based framework, which now provides a broader holistic service lifecycle.

> **Definition: service lifecycle**
>
> An approach to IT service management that emphasizes the importance of coordination and control across the various functions, processes and systems necessary to manage the full lifecycle of IT services. The service lifecycle approach considers the strategy, design, transition, operation and continual improvement of IT services. Also known as service management lifecycle.

The service lifecycle is described in the five ITIL core publications. Each of these covers a stage of the lifecycle (see Figure 1.1), from the initial definition and analysis of business requirements in *ITIL Service Strategy* and *ITIL Service Design*, through migration into the live environment within *ITIL Service Transition*, to live operation and improvement in *ITIL Service Operation* and *ITIL Continual Service Improvement*.

Figure 1.1 The service lifecycle

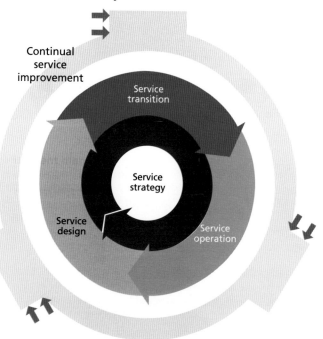

1.3   SERVICE MANAGEMENT

To understand what service management is, we need to understand what services are, and how service management can help service providers to deliver and manage these services.

Definition: service

A means of delivering value to customers by facilitating outcomes customers want to achieve without the ownership of specific costs and risks. The term 'service' is sometimes used as a synonym for core service, IT service or service package.

Definition: IT service

A service provided by an IT service provider. An IT service is made up of a combination of information technology, people and processes. A customer-facing IT service directly supports the business processes of one or more customers and its service level targets should be defined in a service level agreement (SLA). Other IT services, called supporting services, are not directly used by the business but are required by the service provider to deliver customer-facing services.

The outcomes that customers want to achieve are the reason why they purchase or use a service. The value of the service to the customer is directly dependent on how well a service facilitates these outcomes.

Definition: outcome

The result of carrying out an activity, following a process, or delivering an IT service etc. The term is used to refer to intended results as well as to actual results.

Services facilitate outcomes by enhancing the performance of associated tasks and reducing the effect of constraints. These constraints may include regulation, lack of funding or capacity, or technology limitations. The end result is an increase in the probability of desired outcomes. While some services enhance performance of tasks, others have a more direct impact – performing the task itself. Services can be classified as:

- **Core services** These deliver the basic outcomes desired by one or more customers
- **Enabling services** These are needed in order for a core service to be delivered
- **Enhancing services** These are added to core services to make them more appealing to the customer.

Service management enables service providers to:

- Understand the services they are providing
- Ensure that the services really do facilitate the outcomes their customers want to achieve
- Understand the value of the services to their customers
- Understand and manage all of the costs and risks associated with those services.

> **Definition: service management**
>
> A set of specialized organizational capabilities for providing value to customers in the form of services.

These 'specialized organizational capabilities' are described in this guide. They include the processes, activities, functions and roles that service providers use to enable them to deliver services to their customers, as well as the ability to organize, manage knowledge, and understand how to facilitate outcomes that create value. However, service management is more than just a set of capabilities. It is also a professional practice supported by an extensive body of knowledge, experience and skills, with formal schemes for the education, training and certification of practising organizations.

Service management is concerned with more than just delivering services. Each service, process or infrastructure component has a lifecycle, and service management considers the entire lifecycle from strategy through design and transition to operation and continual improvement.

All IT organizations should act as service providers, using the principles of service management to ensure that they deliver the outcomes required by their customers.

> **Definition: IT service management (ITSM)**
>
> The implementation and management of quality IT services that meet the needs of the business. IT service management is performed by IT service providers through an appropriate mix of people, process and information technology.

1.4 PROCESSES AND FUNCTIONS (SO 2.2.2, 2.2.3)

> **Definition: process**
>
> A process is a structured set of activities designed to accomplish a specific objective. A process takes one or more defined inputs and turns them into defined outputs. It may include any of the roles, responsibilities, tools and management controls required to reliably deliver the outputs. A process may define policies, standards, guidelines, activities and work instructions if they are needed.

Processes define actions, dependencies and sequence. Processes have the following characteristics:

■ **Measurability** Processes can be measured and performance-driven, in management terms such as cost and quality, and in practitioner terms such as duration and productivity

■ **Specific results** Processes exist to deliver a specific result that is identifiable and countable

■ **Customers** Processes deliver their primary results to customers or stakeholders, either internal or external, to meet their expectations

■ **Responsiveness to specific triggers** Processes may be ongoing or iterative, but should be traceable to a specific trigger.

The key outputs from any process are driven by the objectives and include process measurement, reports and improvement. For the process to be effective, process outputs have to conform to operational norms derived from business objectives. For the process to be efficient, process activities have to be undertaken with the minimum resources. Figure 1.2 illustrates a process model.

An organization needs to clearly define the roles and responsibilities required to undertake the processes and activities involved in each lifecycle stage. These roles are assigned to individuals within an organizational structure of teams, groups or functions.

Definition: function

A team or group of people and the tools or other resources they use to carry out one or more processes or activities – for example, the service desk.

Figure 1.2 Process model

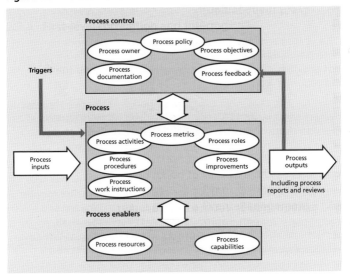

Functions are self-contained, and have the capabilities and resources necessary for their performance and outcomes. They provide organizations with structure and stability. Coordination between functions through shared processes is a common organizational design.

ITIL Service Operation describes the service desk, technical management, IT operations management and application management functions in detail, with technical and application management providing the technical resources and expertise to manage the whole service lifecycle.

1.5   ROLES

A role is a set of responsibilities, activities and authorities granted to a person or team. A role is defined in a process or function. One person or team may have multiple roles. ITIL does not describe all the roles that could possibly exist in an organization, but provides representative examples to aid in an organization's definition of its own roles.

Roles fall into two main categories – generic roles (e.g. process owner) and specific roles that are involved within a particular lifecycle stage or process. Generic roles are described below, while specific roles are covered in the relevant lifecycle chapters of the core ITIL publications.

Note that 'service manager' is a generic term for any manager within the service provider. The term is commonly used to refer to a business relationship manager, a process manager or a senior manager with responsibility for IT services overall. A service manager is often assigned several roles such as business relationship management, service level management and continual service improvement.

1.5.1   Process owner (SO 6.7.2)

The process owner role is accountable for ensuring that a process is fit for purpose, i.e. that it is capable of meeting its objectives; that it is performed according to the agreed and documented standard; and that it meets the aims of the process definition. This role may be assigned to the same person carrying out the process manager role.

Key accountabilities include:

- Sponsoring, designing and change managing the process and its metrics

- Defining the process strategy, with periodic reviews to keep current, and assisting with process design
- Defining appropriate policies and standards for the process, with periodic auditing to ensure compliance
- Communicating process information or changes as appropriate to ensure awareness
- Providing process resources to support activities required throughout the service lifecycle
- Ensuring that process technicians understand their role and have the required knowledge to deliver the process
- Addressing issues with the running of the process
- Identifying enhancement and improvement opportunities and making improvements to the process.

1.5.2 Process manager (SO 6.7.3)

The process manager role is accountable for operational management of a process. There may, for example, be several process managers for one process in different locations. This role may be assigned to the same person carrying out the process owner role.

Key accountabilities include:

- Working with the process owner to plan and coordinate all process activities
- Ensuring that all activities are carried out as required throughout the service lifecycle
- Appointing people to the required roles and managing assigned resources
- Working with service owners and other process managers to ensure the smooth running of services
- Monitoring and reporting on process performance

■ Identifying opportunities for and making improvements to the process.

1.5.3 Process practitioner (SO 6.7.4)

A process practitioner is responsible for carrying out one or more process activities. This role may be assigned to the same person carrying the process manager role, if appropriate.

Responsibilities typically include:

■ Carrying out one or more activities of a process
■ Understanding how his or her role contributes to the overall delivery of service and creation of value for the business
■ Working with other stakeholders, such as line managers, co-workers, users and customers, to ensure that their contributions are effective
■ Ensuring that the inputs, outputs and interfaces for his or her activities are correct
■ Creating or updating records to show that activities have been carried out correctly.

1.5.4 Service owner (SO 6.7.1)

The service owner is responsible to the customer for the initiation, transition and ongoing maintenance and support of a particular service and is accountable to the IT director or service management director for the delivery of a specific IT service. The service owner's accountability for a specific service within an organization is independent of where the underpinning technology components, processes or professional capabilities reside.

Service ownership is critical to service management and one person may fulfil the service owner role for more than one service. Key responsibilities include:

- Ensuring that the ongoing service delivery and support meet agreed customer requirements via effective service monitoring and performance
- Working with business relationship management to ensure that the service provider can meet customer requirements
- Ensuring consistent and appropriate communication with customers for service-related enquiries and issues
- Representing the service across the organization; for example, by attending change advisory board meetings
- Serving as the point of escalation (notification) for major incidents relating to the service
- Participating in internal and external service review meetings
- Participating in negotiating SLAs and operational level agreements (OLAs) relating to the service
- Identifying opportunities for, and making, improvements to the service.

The service owner is responsible for continual improvement and the management of change affecting the service under their care. The service owner is a primary stakeholder in all of the underlying IT processes which enable or support the service they own.

1.5.5   The RACI model (SO 6.8)

Roles are accountable to, or responsible for, an activity. However, as services, processes and their component activities run through an entire organization, each activity must be clearly mapped to well-defined roles. To support this, the RACI model or 'authority matrix' can be used to define the roles and responsibilities in relation to processes and activities.

RACI is an acronym for:

- **Responsible** The person or people responsible for correct execution (i.e. for getting the job done)
- **Accountable** The person who has ownership of quality and the end result. Only one person can be accountable for each task
- **Consulted** The people who are consulted and whose opinions are sought. They have involvement through input of knowledge and information
- **Informed** The people who are kept up to date on progress. They receive information about process execution and quality.

Only one person should be accountable for any process or individual activity, although several people may be responsible for executing parts of the activity.

1.6   OPERATIONAL SUPPORT AND ANALYSIS WITHIN THE CONTEXT OF THE SERVICE LIFECYCLE

1.6.1   Value to the business of operational support and analysis activities (SO 1.1)

Service operation is the stage in the lifecycle where the plans, designs and optimizations are executed and measured. Service operation is where actual value is seen by the business. The value provided to the business by service operation includes:

- Agreed levels of service are consistently delivered to the business enabling the business to gain full value from the service and to improve productivity and quality of business outcomes
- Optimization of the cost and quality of services through reduced unplanned costs and automation

- Operational results and data to support continual service improvement and its investment justification
- Confidence that the IT services are secure and only accessed by those authorized to use them.

1.6.2 OSA within the service lifecycle (SO 1.2.4)

Strategic service objectives are realized through service operation, therefore making it a critical capability.

ITIL Service Operation provides guidance on how to:

- Maintain stability in service operation, allowing for changes in design, scale, scope and service levels
- Achieve effectiveness and efficiency across two major control perspectives: reactive and proactive
- Enable better decision-making in areas such as managing availability, controlling demand, optimizing capacity utilization, scheduling operations, and avoiding or resolving service incidents and managing problems.

1.6.3 Optimizing service operation performance (SO 3.1.2)

Service operation is optimized in two ways:

- Long-term incremental improvement based on evaluating the performance and output of all service operation processes, functions and outputs over time. This type of improvement is typically driven by the continual service improvement stage
- Short-term ongoing improvement of working practices within the service operation processes, functions and technology. These are generally smaller improvements that can be implemented without any fundamental impact.

2 Event management

2.1 PURPOSE AND OBJECTIVES (SO 4.1.1)

The purpose of event management is to manage events throughout their lifecycle. This lifecycle detects events, makes sense of them and determines the appropriate control action, all of which are coordinated by the event management process.

Event management is therefore the basis for operational monitoring and control. If events are programmed to communicate operational information as well as warnings and exceptions, they can be used as a basis for automating many routine operations management activities.

The objectives of the event management process are to:

- Detect all changes of state that have significance for the management of a configuration item (CI) or IT service
- Determine the appropriate action for events and ensure communication to the appropriate functions
- Provide the trigger for the execution of many processes and operations management activities
- Provide comparison of actual operating performance against design standards and service level agreements (SLAs)
- Provide a basis for service assurance, reporting and service improvement.

2.2 SCOPE (SO 4.1.2)

Event management can be applied to any aspect of service management that needs to be controlled and can be automated. This includes:

- Configuration items (CIs): monitoring of CIs to confirm they remain in a required state or automating frequent changing of a CI state, and updating the configuration management system (CMS) accordingly
- Environmental conditions
- Software licence monitoring to ensure optimum and legal licence utilization and allocation
- Security
- Normal activity such as tracking usage or performance.

Event management and monitoring are closely related but different. Event management generates and detects specific notifications for monitoring, whereas monitoring detects and tracks these notifications but also actively monitors conditions that do not generate events; for example, to check that devices are operating within acceptable limits.

2.3   VALUE TO THE BUSINESS AND SERVICE LIFECYCLE (SO 4.1.3)

Event management typically provides indirect value to the business, which can be determined on the basis of the following:

- Early detection of incidents, often leading to assignment for resolution prior to any actual service outage
- Enabling automated activities to be managed by exception, reducing the need for costly real-time monitoring and downtime
- Integration into other service management processes, which can enable detection and notification of status changes or exceptions, triggering an early response and improving process performance
- Automated operations, which increase efficiency and reduce the need for expensive human resources.

2.4   POLICIES, PRINCIPLES AND BASIC CONCEPTS (SO 4.1.4)

Examples of event management policies might include:

- Event notifications should go only to those responsible for the handling of their actions, with event routing information being constantly maintained
- Event management and support should be centralized as much as reasonably possible
- Changes and additions for the rule base will need to be under the control of change management
- Common messaging and logging standards and protocols should be used
- Event handling actions should be automated wherever possible
- There should be a standard classification scheme referencing common handling and escalation processes. Notification of incidents and problems should be aligned to the organization's existing categorization and prioritization policies
- All recognized events should be captured and logged, available for data manipulation, filtering and reporting to support incident and problem diagnosis activities.

2.4.1 Types of event

There are three types of event:

- **Informational** This is an event not requiring action, usually logged and retained for an agreed time. It is typically used in regular operations to check that a device or service status or activity has been completed (e.g. a notification that a scheduled task has finished or a user has logged in). This type of event can be used to generate activity statistics

- **Warning** This is an unusual but not exceptional operation, usually when a device is approaching a threshold, indicating closer monitoring or checking is required. This type of situation may either resolve itself or require operator intervention; for example, if the completion time for a transaction is 10% longer than normal. These rules or policies are defined in the monitoring and control objectives for the device or server
- **Exception** This is when a service or device is operating abnormally and action is required: for example, an attempted logon with the incorrect password; a device with an unacceptable utilization rate; or a service that is down. This may mean an SLA and an operational level agreement (OLA) have been breached and the business impacted.

2.4.2 Filtering of events

Filtering enables focused management and control of significant events. Strategies for filtering include:

- Integrating filtering into service management processes
- Designing new services that consider event management
- Formally evaluating the effectiveness of filtering
- Planning for the deployment of event management across the entire IT infrastructure.

2.4.3 Designing for event management (SO 4.1.4.3)

Design for event management should take place during the design of a service supported by service operations functions. Event management is the basis for monitoring service performance and availability against targets agreed during the availability and capacity management processes. The designed events should then be tested and evaluated during service transition.

Once event management has been deployed, day-to-day operations may identify additional events and other improvements through continual improvement.

Key design considerations include:

- What needs to be monitored?
- What type of monitoring is required?
- When should an event be generated?
- What information needs communicating?
- Who are the messages intended for?
- Who will be responsible for handling the event?

Specific design areas include:

- **Instrumentation** Defining and designing how to monitor and control the IT infrastructure and services. Mechanisms to be designed include event generation, classification, communication, escalation, logging and storage
- **Error messaging** Providing meaningful error messages and codes within software applications for inclusion in events
- **Event detection and alert mechanisms** Designing and populating tools with the criteria and rules to filter, correlate and escalate events. Design of event detection and alert mechanisms requires knowledge of:
  - Business processes and service level requirements
  - Who is going to support the CI and what they need to know to support the event and diagnose problems
  - Normal and abnormal operation levels and the significance of repeat events
  - CI dependencies and relationships
  - Significance of multiple similar events.

2.4.4 Event rule sets and correlation engines (SO 4.1.4.4)

A rule set consists of a number of rules that define how the event messages for a specific event will be processed and evaluated. The rules are typically embedded into monitoring and event handling technologies, consisting of algorithms which correlate events that have been generated (e.g. CI state changes) to create logical additional events that need to be communicated (e.g. service or business impact events). These algorithms can be coded into event management tools referred to as correlation engines.

2.5 PROCESS ACTIVITIES, METHODS AND TECHNIQUES (SO 4.1.5)

2.5.1 Event occurrence

Events occur continuously but not all are detected or registered. It is therefore important that those which need to be detected are understood so they can be appropriately designed and managed (see Figure 2.1).

2.5.2 Event notification

There are two ways in which notification of events can take place:

- A management tool interrogates devices to collect data, i.e. polling
- CIs generate notifications under predefined conditions that were designed and built into the CI.

Service design should define which events need to be generated and, for each CI, specify how this should be done. During service transition, event generation is set up and tested. In many organizations, a standard set of events is used initially and tuned over time.

Figure 2.1 The event management process

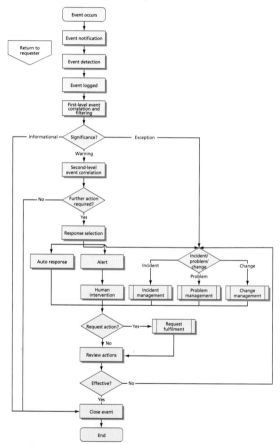

Decision-making about events is much easier when meaningful data, targeted for a specific audience, is included in event notifications.

2.5.3 Event detection

Event notifications are detected by an agent running on the same system or by a management tool.

2.5.4 Event logging

All events should be recorded, either as an event record or as an entry in the systems log. Where system logs are used they need to be routinely and regularly checked with instructions for any actions required. Event management procedures need to define how long events and logs are kept before being archived.

2.5.5 First-level correlation and filtering

This stage determines whether to communicate an event or ignore it. Ignored events are typically logged with no further action.

Filtering eliminates duplicates and unwanted events that cannot be disabled.

Filtering undertakes the initial level of 'correlation', i.e. an assessment of whether the event is informational, a warning or an exception. Filtering is not always necessary; for some CIs every event is significant and events go straight to event correlation.

2.5.6 Event significance

Events need to be categorized: recommended categories are 'informational', 'warning' and 'exception', as described in section 2.4.

2.5.7   Second-level event correlation

The meaning of the event is normally determined by the correlation engine which compares the event with a set of criteria (called business rules) in a predefined order to establish the level and type of business impact. The correlation engine is programmed in line with the performance standards defined during service design, plus any additional guidance specific to the operating environment, such as the number of similar events or a comparison of utilization information in the event of reaching minimum or maximum thresholds.

2.5.8   Action and response selection

If the correlation activity recognizes an event, a response is required. The action initiates the appropriate response.

At this point one or more responses can be chosen in any combination. Figure 2.1 shows some options. Options include:

■ Auto-responses generated for defined events where the response will initiate the action and then evaluate whether it was completed successfully, such as when rebooting a device

■ An alert raised for human intervention, containing all the information necessary for the person to determine the appropriate action

■ Incident, problem and/or change records generated:
  – Incident records can be generated immediately when an exception is detected or as determined by the correlation engine, including as much information about the event as possible
  – Problem records are typically updated to link an incident to an existing problem

– Requests for change (RFCs) can be generated immediately when an exception is detected or when correlation identifies that a change is needed.

2.5.9 Event review

Because of the high volumes involved, not all events can be formally reviewed. However, significant events or exceptions do need to be reviewed and trends monitored. Reviews should not duplicate any other reviews done as part of other processes such as change management. They should check that events have been handled properly and that the handover between event management and the other processes is effective.

Event reviews also provide input into continual improvement, and the evaluation and audit of the event management process.

2.5.10 Event closure

Most events are not 'opened' or 'closed'; informational events are only logged. Auto-response events are typically closed by the generation of a second event, triggered on completion of the action initiated. Events linked to incidents, problems or changes are formally closed with a link to the relevant record from the other process.

2.6 TRIGGERS, INPUTS, OUTPUTS AND INTERFACES (SO 4.1.6)

Triggers include:

- Exceptions to any level of CI performance defined in the design specifications, OLAs or standard operating procedures
- Exceptions to an automated procedure or process

- An exception within a business process monitored by event management
- Completion of an automated task or job
- A status change in a server or database CI
- Access of an application or database by a user or automated procedure or job
- A predefined threshold is reached; for example, by a device, database or application.

Inputs include:

- Operational and service level requirements associated with events
- Alarms, alerts and thresholds for recognizing events
- Event correlation tables, rules, event codes and automated response solutions
- Roles and responsibilities for recognizing and communicating events
- Operational procedures for recognizing, logging, escalating and communicating events.

Outputs include:

- Events communications and escalations
- Event logs
- Events that indicate an incident has occurred
- Events that indicate the potential breach of an SLA or OLA objective
- Events and alerts that indicate completion status of deployment, operational or other support activities
- A service knowledge management system (SKMS) populated with event information and history.

Event management can interface with any process that requires monitoring and control. Examples of interfacing include:

- **Service level management (SLM)** Ensures that any event with potential impact on SLAs is detected early and any failures are rectified as soon as possible
- **Information security management** Allows potentially significant business security events to be detected and acted upon
- **Capacity and availability management** Defines significant events, thresholds and responses for event management to monitor, detect and respond to when they occur. Also event management should produce reports on patterns of events and potential areas of improvement
- **Service asset and configuration management** Uses events to determine the current status of CIs in the infrastructure
- **Knowledge management** Processes events for inclusion in knowledge management systems. For example, patterns of performance can be correlated with business activity and used as input into future design and strategy decisions
- **Change management** Interfaces with event management to identify conditions that may require a response or action
- **Incident and problem management** Requires information on events that may require a response or action to resolve incidents and problems
- **Access management** Events can be used to detect unauthorized access attempts and security breaches.

2.7   INFORMATION MANAGEMENT (SO 4.1.7)

The following information is used in event management:

- Simple network management protocol (SNMP) messages: a standard way of communicating technical information about the status of components of an IT infrastructure
- Management information bases (MIBs) of IT devices: an MIB is the database on each device that contains information about that device, including, for example, its operating system and configuration of system parameters. The ability to interrogate MIBs and compare them to a norm is critical to being able to generate events
- Vendor's monitoring software
- Correlation engines containing detailed rules to determine the significance and appropriate response to events
- Event records for all types of event: the format and content depend on the tool being used, but typically include the device, component, type of failure, date and time, parameters in exception, unique identifier and value.

2.8   CRITICAL SUCCESS FACTORS AND KEY PERFORMANCE INDICATORS (SO 4.1.8)

The efficiency and effectiveness of the process can be measured by identifying critical success factors (CSFs) for the process, each CSF being supported by key performance indicators (KPIs):

- **CSF** Detecting all changes of state that have significance for the management of CIs and IT services:
  - **KPI** Number and ratio of events compared with the number of incidents

- **KPI** Number and percentage of each type of event per platform or application versus total number of platforms and applications underpinning live IT services (looking to identify IT services that may be at risk for lack of capability to detect their events)

■ **CSF** Ensuring all events are communicated to the appropriate functions that need to be informed or take further control actions:
  - **KPI** Number and percentage of events that required human intervention and whether this was performed
  - **KPI** Number of incidents that occurred and percentage of these that were triggered without a corresponding event

■ **CSF** Providing the trigger, or entry point, for the execution of many service operation processes and operations management activities:
  - **KPI** Number and percentage of events that required human intervention and whether this was performed

■ **CSF** Provide the means to compare actual operating performance and behaviour against design standards and SLAs:
  - **KPI** Number and percentage of incidents that were resolved without impact to the business (indicates the overall effectiveness of the event management process and underpinning solutions)
  - **KPI** Number and percentage of events that resulted in incidents or changes
  - **KPI** Number and percentage of events caused by existing problems or known errors (this may result in a change to the priority of work on that problem or known error)
  - **KPI** Number and percentage of events indicating performance issues (for example, growth in the number of times an application exceeded its transaction thresholds over the past six months)

- **KPI** Number and percentage of events indicating potential availability issues (e.g. failovers to alternative devices, or excessive workload swapping)
- **CSF** Providing a basis for service assurance, reporting and service improvement:
  - **KPI** Number and percentage of repeated or duplicated events (this will help in the tuning of the correlation engine to eliminate unnecessary event generation and can also be used to assist in the design of better event generation functionality in new services)
  - **KPI** Number of events/alerts generated without actual degradation of service/functionality (false positives – indication of the accuracy of the instrumentation parameters, important for continual service improvement).

2.9   CHALLENGES AND RISKS (SO 4.1.9)

Challenges include the following:

- Difficulty of obtaining funding for the necessary tools and effort needed to install them and exploit their benefits
- Setting the correct level of filtering
- Difficulty and high cost of deploying the necessary monitoring agents across the entire IT infrastructure
- The additional network traffic generated by automated monitoring activities might have negative impacts on the planned capacity levels of the network
- Time needed to acquire the necessary skills, and high cost
- Setting up the necessary processes in order to deploy the event management tools.

Risks include:

- Failure to obtain adequate funding
- Ensuring an incorrect level of filtering
- Failure to maintain momentum in deploying monitoring agents across the IT infrastructure.

2.10   ROLES AND RESPONSIBILITIES (SO 6.7.8)

2.10.1 Event management process owner

Responsibilities include:

- Carrying out the generic process owner role for the event management process (see section 1.5 for more detail)
- Planning and managing support for event management tools and processes
- Working with other process owners to ensure an integrated approach to the design and implementation of event, incident, request fulfilment, access and problem management.

2.10.2 Event management process manager

Responsibilities include:

- Carrying out the generic process manager role for the event management process (see section 1.5 for more detail)
- Planning and managing support for event management tools and processes
- Coordinating interfaces between event management and other service management processes.

2.10.3 Other event management roles

The service desk is not typically involved in event management, unless an event requires some response that is within the scope of the service desk's defined activity, such as notifying a user that a report is ready. Generally, this type of activity is performed by the operations bridge, unless the service desk and operations bridge have been combined.

However, for events identified as incidents the service desk is responsible for:

- Investigation and resolution of events identified as incidents and then escalation to the appropriate service operation team
- Communication of information about this type of incident to the relevant technical or application management team and, where appropriate, the user.

Technical and application management staff play several important roles:

- During service design: participation in designing the warranty aspects of the service such as classifying events, updating correlation engines, or ensuring that any auto-responses are defined
- During service transition: testing the service to ensure that events are properly generated and that the defined responses are appropriate
- During service operation: performing event management for the systems under their control; dealing with incidents and problems related to events
- If event management activities are delegated, ensuring that the staff are adequately trained and that they have access to the appropriate tools to enable them to perform these tasks.

IT operations management staff fulfil the following roles:

- Event monitoring and first-line response may be delegated to IT operations management
- Event monitoring is commonly delegated to the operations bridge where it exists. The operations bridge can coordinate or perform the responses required or provide first-level support.

3   Incident management

3.1   PURPOSE AND OBJECTIVES (SO 4.2.1)

The primary goal of the incident management process is to restore normal service operation as quickly as possible and minimize the adverse impact on business operations, ensuring that agreed levels of service quality are maintained. 'Normal service operation' is defined here as an operational state where services and CIs are performing within the agreed service and operational levels.

The objectives of the incident management process are to:

- Ensure that standardized methods and procedures are used for efficient and prompt response, analysis, documentation, ongoing management and reporting of incidents
- Increase visibility and communication of incidents to business and IT support staff
- Enhance business perception of IT through use of a professional approach in quickly resolving and communicating incidents when they occur
- Align incident management activities and priorities with those of the business
- Maintain user satisfaction with the quality of IT services.

3.2   SCOPE (SO 4.2.2)

Incident management includes any event that disrupts, or which could disrupt, a service. This includes events communicated directly by users through the service desk or detected through an interface from event management to incident management tools and/or logged by technical staff.

Not all events are incidents. Many classes of events are not related to disruptions at all, but are indicators of normal operation or are simply informational (see section 2.3).

Similarly, although incidents and service requests are both reported to the service desk, service requests do not represent a disruption to the agreed service and so are not within the scope of incident management, as they are dealt with by the request fulfilment process.

3.3 VALUE TO THE BUSINESS AND SERVICE LIFECYCLE (SO 4.2.3)

The value of incident management includes the ability to:

- Reduce unplanned labour and costs for both the business and IT support staff
- Detect and resolve incidents resulting in lower downtime and higher service availability
- Identify business priorities and dynamically allocate resources to incidents based on real-time business priorities
- Identify potential improvements to services by understanding what constitutes an incident and aligning with the activities of business operational staff
- Identify additional service or training requirements found in IT or the business.

Incident management is highly visible to the business, and it is therefore easier to demonstrate its value than most areas in service operation. For this reason, incident management is often one of the first processes to be implemented in service management projects. The added benefit of doing this is that incident management can be used to highlight other areas that need attention – thereby providing a justification for expenditure on implementing other processes.

3.4   POLICIES, PRINCIPLES AND BASIC CONCEPTS (SO 4.2.4)

Examples of incident management policies might include:

■ Incidents and statuses must be communicated in a timely and effective way

■ All incident records must have a common format and set of information fields; there must be common and agreed criteria for prioritizing and escalating incidents; and a standard classification schema for incidents must be adopted

■ Incidents must be resolved within timeframes acceptable to the business, be aligned with overall service levels and objectives, and maintain customer satisfaction

■ All incidents must be stored and managed in a single management system, integrated with other service management technologies that use or provide incident information. Status and detailed information on the incident must be recorded and updated on a timely basis in incident records

■ Incident records must be audited on a regular basis to ensure they have been entered and categorized correctly, with feedback mechanisms to communicate audit findings and issues to incident-handling staff.

3.4.1   Timescales

Timescales must be agreed for all incident-handling stages, based on the overall incident response and resolution targets within service level agreements (SLAs) and captured as targets within operational level agreements (OLAs) and underpinning contracts (UCs). All support groups need to be made aware of these timescales. Service management tools can be used to automate timescales and escalate the incident as required, based on predefined rules.

3.4.2 Incident models

Organizations can predefine 'standard' incident models and apply them to appropriate incidents when they occur.

An incident model is a way of setting out the steps required to handle a particular type of incident in an agreed way. This ensures that 'standard' incidents are handled in a predefined way and within predefined timescales.

The incident model includes:

- The steps to take to handle the incident, the sequence, dependencies and responsibilities
- Timescales and thresholds for completion of the actions; escalation procedures
- Any necessary evidence-preservation activities (particularly relevant for security and capacity-related incidents).

The models are input to the incident-handling support tools, which then automate the handling, management and escalation of the process.

3.4.3 Major incidents

A definition of what constitutes a major incident must be agreed and, ideally, mapped onto the overall incident prioritization system.

A specific procedure, with shorter timescales and greater urgency, must be used for 'major' incidents. A separate major incident team may be formed, under the direct leadership of the incident manager, as necessary. If the service desk manager is also fulfilling the role of incident manager, then a separate person may need to lead the major incident investigation team, ultimately reporting back to the incident manager.

Sometimes, a major incident is defined erroneously as a problem. In reality, an incident remains an incident forever – it may grow in impact or priority to become a major incident, in which case it triggers a root cause analysis to find the underlying cause and to avoid recurrence. A problem, on the other hand, always remains a separate entity.

3.4.4   Incident status tracking

Incidents should be tracked throughout their lifecycle to support proper handling and reporting on the status of incidents. Within the incident management system, status codes may be linked to incidents to indicate where they are in relation to the lifecycle. Examples include 'open', 'in progress', 'resolved' and 'closed'.

3.4.5   Expanded incident lifecycle

ITIL Service Design and *ITIL Continual Service Improvement* describe the expanded incident lifecycle which can be used to help understand all contributions to the impact of incidents and to plan for how these could be controlled or reduced.

3.5   PROCESS ACTIVITIES, METHODS AND TECHNIQUES (SO 4.2.5)

The process to be followed during the management of an incident is shown in Figure 3.1.

Figure 3.1 Incident management process flow

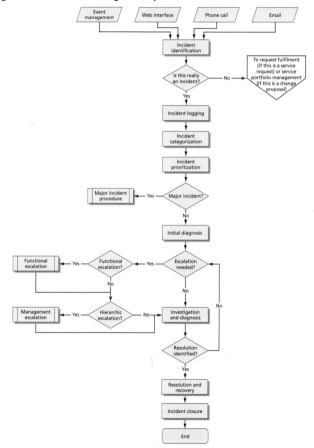

The check for service requests in this process does not imply that service requests are incidents. Service requests may be incorrectly logged as incidents (e.g. a user wrongly enters the request as an incident from the web interface). This check detects any such requests and ensures that they are passed to the request fulfilment process.

3.5.1 Incident identification

As far as possible, all key components need to be monitored so that failures or potential failures are detected early, initiating incident management and, ideally, enabling incident resolution before they have an impact on users. See Chapter 2 for further details.

3.5.2 Incident logging

All incidents must be fully logged and date- and/or time-stamped, regardless of whether they are raised through a service desk telephone call, automatically detected via an event alert or identified in any other way.

All relevant information relating to the nature of the incident must be logged so that the details are available for other support groups, if required. The incident record is updated throughout the process. Details logged may include:

- Unique reference number
- Incident categorization, urgency, impact and prioritization
- Date and/or time recorded and name or ID of the person and/or group recording the incident
- Method of notification (e.g. telephone, automatic, email, in person) and call-back method (e.g. telephone, mail)
- Description of symptoms
- Incident status (e.g. active, waiting, closed)

- Related CI, problem, known error
- Support group or person the incident is allocated to
- Activities undertaken to resolve the incident
- Resolution date and/or time
- Closure category and date and/or time.

All staff involved in logging incidents, such as IT operations or network support, need to be trained in logging procedures and information.

3.5.3 Incident categorization

Initial logging must allocate suitable incident categorization coding so that the exact type of call is recorded. This is important to establish trends of incident types and frequencies for use in problem management, supplier management and other ITSM activities.

Multi-level categorization is available in most tools – usually to three or four levels of granularity. An example of multi-level incident categorization is shown in Figure 3.2.

Figure 3.2 Multi-level incident categorization

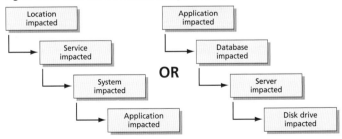

There is no generic guidance on the categories an organization should use. Where no categories exist, a practical approach is to establish an initial set of top-level categorizations, with an 'other' category. After a trial period, analysis of incidents logged can help to identify improved categories and determine the lower-level categories required. These activities can be repeated after a further period, and again regularly, to ensure that they remain relevant. Since any significant changes to categorization may cause some difficulties for incident trending or management reporting, they should be stabilized unless changes are genuinely required.

Categorization of the incident must be checked, and updated if necessary, at call closure time (in a separate closure categorization field, so as not to corrupt the original categorization).

3.5.4 Incident prioritization

For every incident an appropriate prioritization code must be agreed and allocated, as this determines how the incident is handled by support tools and support staff.

Prioritization can normally be determined by taking into account the urgency of the incident (how quickly the business needs a resolution) and the level of impact it is causing. An indication of impact is often (but not always) the number of users being affected. However, the loss of service to a single user can have a major business impact. Other factors that also contribute to impact levels are:

■ Risk to life or limb
■ The number of services affected – may be multiple services
■ The level of financial losses
■ Effect on business reputation
■ Regulatory or legislative breaches.

An effective way of calculating these elements and deriving an overall priority level for each incident is given in Table 3.1.

Table 3.1 Simple priority coding system

Impact					
		High	Medium	Low	
	High	1	2	3	
	Medium	2	3	4	
	Low	3	4	5	
Priority code				Description	Target resolution time
1				Critical	1 hour
2				High	8 hours
3				Medium	24 hours
4				Low	48 hours
5				Planning	Planned

Clear guidance must be provided to enable all support staff to determine the correct urgency and impact levels, so that the correct priority can be allocated. Such guidance needs to be produced during service level negotiations.

However, there may be occasions when normal priority levels have to be overridden; for example, because of particular business expediency. The service desk should comply with such requests and correct priority levels later rather than dispute them with the user.

Organizations may also recognize 'very important people' (VIPs): high-ranking executives, officers, diplomats, politicians etc. whose incidents are handled on a higher priority than normal. VIPs need to be documented in the guidance provided to the service desk staff.

An incident's priority may be dynamic; if circumstances change, or if an incident is not resolved within SLA target times, ensure the priority is updated as required to reflect the new situation.

3.5.5   Initial diagnosis

For incidents routed via the service desk, a service desk analyst carries out initial diagnosis, typically while the user is still on the telephone, to try to discover the full symptoms of the incident, determine exactly what has gone wrong and decide how to correct it. At this stage, diagnostic scripts and known error information enable early and accurate diagnosis. Where the resolution is successful, the incident is closed.

Where a service desk analyst cannot resolve an incident while talking to the user but feels that the service desk may be able to do so within the agreed time limit without assistance from other support groups, the analyst informs the user of their intentions, gives the user an incident reference number and attempts to find a resolution.

3.5.6   Incident escalation

There are two types of incident escalation:

- ■ **Functional escalation** If the service desk is unable to resolve the incident or if target times for first-point resolution have been exceeded, whichever comes first, the incident must be immediately escalated for further support. Escalation is either to a second-level support group or to an appropriate third-level support group (where the second-level group has not been able to resolve the incident within agreed target times or deeper technical knowledge is required).

Third-level support groups may be internal or third parties, with the rules for escalation and handling of incidents agreed in OLAs and UCs.

Regardless of where an incident is referred to during its life, ownership of the incident remains with the service desk at all times. The service desk remains responsible for tracking progress, keeping users informed and ultimately for incident closure.

- ■ **Hierarchic escalation** If incidents are serious (e.g. Priority 1) the appropriate IT managers and relevant customer managers must be notified, for informational purposes at least. Hierarchic escalation is also used if the 'investigation and diagnosis' and 'resolution and recovery' steps are taking too long or proving too difficult. Hierarchic escalation continues up the management chain so that senior managers are aware and can be prepared to take any necessary action; for example, allocating additional resources or involving suppliers and maintainers.

  Hierarchic escalation is used when there is contention over to whom the incident is allocated.

  IT senior managers need to keep customer managers informed of the status of progress and expected time of resolution and next communication.

The levels and timescales for functional and hierarchic escalation need to be agreed, taking into account SLA targets, and embedded within support tools, which then police and control the process flow within agreed timescales.

The service desk keeps the user informed of any relevant escalation that takes place and ensures the incident record is updated to keep a full history of actions.

If there are many incidents in a queue with the same priority level, the service desk and/or incident management staff initially decide the order in which the incidents are picked up and worked on, in conjunction with the managers of the relevant support groups. These managers must ensure that incidents are dealt with in true business priority order and that staff are not allowed to 'cherry-pick' the incidents.

3.5.7 Investigation and diagnosis

Support groups investigate and diagnose what has gone wrong and document all activities (including details of any actions taken to try to resolve or recreate the incident) in the incident record to maintain a complete record of all activities.

Investigations may include:

- Establishing exactly what has gone wrong or what is being sought by the user
- Understanding the chronological order of events
- Confirming the full impact of the incident, including the number and/or range of users affected
- Identifying any events that could have triggered the incident (e.g. a recent change or user action)
- Knowledge searches for previous occurrences by searching incident and problem records and/or known error databases, manufacturers' and suppliers' error logs or knowledge databases.

Where possible, perform these activities in parallel to reduce overall timescales.

3.5.8 Resolution and recovery

When a potential resolution has been identified, this is applied and tested. Specific actions and the people involved may vary depending on the fault.

When a resolution has been found, sufficient testing must be performed to ensure that the recovery action is complete and that the service has been fully restored to the users.

The incident record must be updated with all relevant information and details, regardless of the actions taken or who does them, to maintain a full history.

The resolving group passes the incident back to the service desk for closure action.

3.5.9 Incident closure

The service desk checks that the incident is fully resolved and that the users are satisfied and agree the incident can be closed. The service desk also undertakes:

- **Closure categorization** Confirms that the initial incident categorization was correct or, if incorrect, updates the record with correct closure categorization, taking advice from the resolving group as necessary
- **User satisfaction survey** A user satisfaction call-back or email survey for an agreed percentage of incidents
- **Incident documentation** Ensures that the incident record is fully documented, resolving any outstanding areas
- **Ongoing or recurring problem** Determines (in conjunction with resolver groups) the likelihood of incident recurrence and whether any preventive action is necessary to avoid this, raising a problem record in conjunction with problem management
- **Formal closure** Formally closes the incident record.

Organizations may have an automatic closure period on specific, or even all, incidents (e.g. after two working days if no further contact is made by the user). This approach must always be discussed and agreed with the users, and publicized.

Incidents may, on occasion, recur even though formally closed. To cope with this, determine predefined rules for if, or when, an incident can be reopened. For example, if an incident recurs within one working day it can be reopened, but beyond this a new incident must be raised, linked to the previous incident.

The exact time threshold and rules may vary from one organization to another – but clear rules need to be agreed and documented, and guidance given to all service desk staff and consistently applied.

3.6   TRIGGERS, INPUTS, OUTPUTS AND INTERFACES (SO 4.2.6)

Triggers include the following:

- A user rings the service desk or completes a web-based incident-logging screen
- Event management tools trigger the incident automatically
- Technical staff identify potential failures and raise an incident themselves or via the service desk
- A supplier notifies the service desk of a potential or actual difficulty needing attention.

Inputs include:

- Information about CIs and their status
- Information about known errors and workarounds
- Communication about incidents and their symptoms

- Communication about requests for change (RFCs) and releases
- Communication of events
- Operational and service level objectives
- Customer feedback
- Agreed criteria for prioritizing and escalating incidents.

Outputs include:

- Resolved incidents and resolution actions
- Updated incident management records
- Problem records
- Feedback on incidents related to changes and releases
- Identification of CIs associated with or impacted by incidents
- Satisfaction feedback.

Interfaces include:

- **Service level management (SLM)** Requires a process that can resolve incidents in a specified time, and can provide information and reports that enable SLM to review services and identify service weaknesses and improvements. SLM defines the acceptable levels of service within which incident management works, including:
  - Impact definitions
  - Incident response, progress update and target fix times
  - Service definitions, which are mapped to users
  - Rules for requesting services

  Incident management enables SLM to define measurable responses to service disruptions, providing reports that enable SLM to review SLAs. Incident management supports identification of areas where services are weak, so that SLM can define actions as part of the service improvement plan

- **Information security management** Requires information on security incidents to measure the effectiveness of security measures and support service design activities
- **Capacity management** Incident management provides a trigger for performance monitoring where there appears to be a performance problem. Capacity management may develop workarounds for incidents
- **Availability management** Incident management data can be used to determine the availability of IT services and establish where the incident lifecycle can be improved
- **Service asset and configuration management** Provides data to identify and progress incidents. The configuration management system (CMS) also contains information about which categories of incident are assigned to which support group. In turn, incident management can maintain the status of faulty CIs and support configuration management audits of the infrastructure when working to resolve an incident
- **Change management** Changes required to implement workarounds or resolutions need to be logged as RFCs and progressed through change management. In turn, incident management detects and resolves incidents arising from failed changes
- **Problem management** Provides known errors and workarounds for faster incident resolution and also the investigation and resolution of the underlying cause of incidents preventing or reducing the impact of recurrence
- **Access management** Requires information on unauthorized access attempts and security breaches.

3.7 INFORMATION MANAGEMENT (SO 4.2.7)

Most information used in incident management comes from the following sources:

- **Incident management tools** Containing information about incident and problem history, incident categories, action taken to resolve, and diagnostic scripts
- **CMS** Helping to identify the CIs affected by the incident and also to estimate the impact of the incident
- **Known error database** Providing valuable information about possible resolutions and workarounds, discussed in section 5.5.7.

Incident management in turn generates the following information:

- Incident records, including the data listed in section 3.5.2
- Incident details serving as inputs to problem records.

3.8 CRITICAL SUCCESS FACTORS AND KEY PERFORMANCE INDICATORS (SO 4.2.8)

The efficiency and effectiveness of the process can be measured by identifying critical success factors (CSFs) for the process, each CSF being supported by key performance indicators (KPIs):

- **CSF** Resolve incidents as quickly as possible, minimizing impacts to the business:
  - **KPI** Mean elapsed time to achieve incident resolution or circumvention, broken down by impact code
  - **KPI** Breakdown of incidents at each stage (e.g. logged, work in progress, closed)
  - **KPI** Percentage of incidents closed by the service desk without reference to other levels of support (often referred to as 'first point of contact')

- – **KPI** Number and percentage of incidents resolved remotely, without the need for a visit
- – **KPI** Number of incidents resolved without impact to the business (e.g. incident was raised by event management and resolved before it could impact the business)
- ■ **CSF** Maintain quality of IT services:
  - – **KPI** Total numbers of incidents (as a control measure)
  - – **KPI** Size of current incident backlog for each IT service
  - – **KPI** Number and percentage of major incidents for each IT service
- ■ **CSF** Maintain user satisfaction with IT services
  - – **KPI** Average user or customer survey score (total and by question category)
  - – **KPI** Percentage of satisfaction surveys answered versus total number of satisfaction surveys sent
- ■ **CSF** Increase visibility and communication of incidents to business and IT support staff:
  - – **KPI** Average number of service desk calls or other contacts from business users for incidents already reported
  - – **KPI** Number of business user complaints or issues about the content and quality of incident communications
- ■ **CSF** Align incident management activities and priorities with those of the business:
  - – **KPI** Percentage of incidents handled within agreed response time (incident response-time targets may be specified in SLAs, for example, by impact and urgency codes)
  - – **KPI** Average cost per incident

- **CSF** Ensure that standardized methods and procedures are used for efficient and prompt response, analysis, documentation, ongoing management and reporting of incidents to maintain business confidence in IT capabilities:
  - **KPI** Number and percentage of incidents incorrectly assigned
  - **KPI** Number and percentage of incidents incorrectly categorized
  - **KPI** Number and percentage of incidents processed per service desk agent
  - **KPI** Number and percentage of incidents related to changes and releases.

A breakdown and categorization of incident metrics by category, timeframe, impact, urgency, service impacted, location and priority provides input to problem management, continual service improvement and other processes to identify issues, problem trends or other situations.

3.9   CHALLENGES AND RISKS (SO 4.2.9)

Challenges include:

- The ability to detect incidents as early as possible
- Convincing all staff that all incidents must be logged, encouraging the use of self-help facilities
- Availability of information about problems and known errors
- Integration with the CMS and use of CI relationships and CI histories
- Integration with the SLM process, to correctly assess the impact and priority of incidents and assist in the use of escalation procedures.

Risks include:

- Being inundated with incidents that cannot be handled within acceptable timescales due to a lack of available or properly trained resources
- Unintended backlog of incidents created by inadequate support tools
- Lack of adequate or timely information sources because of poor tools or lack of integration
- Mismatches in objectives or actions due to poorly aligned or absent OLAs and/or UCs.

3.10 ROLES AND RESPONSIBILITIES (SO 6.7.5)

3.10.1 Incident management process owner

Responsibilities include:

- Carrying out the generic process owner role for the incident management process (see section 1.5)
- Designing incident models and workflows
- Ensuring there is an integrated approach to incident management, problem management, event management, access management and request fulfilment.

3.10.2 Incident management process manager

Responsibilities include:

- Carrying out the generic process manager role for the incident management process (see section 1.5)
- Planning and managing support for incident management tools and processes, coordinating interfaces with other service management processes

■ Producing management information
■ Managing the work of incident support staff (first- and second-line)
■ Monitoring and driving the effectiveness of incident management and making recommendations for improvement
■ Developing and maintaining the incident management systems and processes
■ Managing major incidents.

The role of incident manager may be assigned to the service desk supervisor.

3.10.3 First-line analyst

This role is that of providing first-line support for incidents and is often combined with the service desk analyst:

■ Recording, providing ownership, monitoring, tracking and communication for incidents
■ Providing resolution and recovery of incidents or routeing incidents to specialist support groups
■ Analysing for correct prioritization, classification and providing initial support
■ Keeping users and the service desk informed about incident progress
■ Escalating incidents as necessary per established escalation policies
■ Closing incidents.

3.10.4 Second-line analyst

A second-line support group is typically made up of staff with greater (though still general) technical skills than the service desk. They have additional time to devote to incident diagnosis and resolution without interference from telephone interruptions. Key responsibilities are similar to the first-line analyst role.

3.10.5 Third-line analyst

Third-line support can be provided by internal technical groups and/or third-party suppliers including network, voice, server, desktop, application management, database, hardware maintenance engineers and environmental equipment maintainers or suppliers.

4 Request fulfilment

4.1 PURPOSE AND OBJECTIVES (SO 4.3.1)

Request fulfilment is the process responsible for managing all service requests from the users through their lifecycle.

The objectives of the request fulfilment process are to:

- Maintain user and customer satisfaction by handling all service requests in an efficient and professional manner
- Provide a channel for users to request and receive standard services for which there is a predefined authorization and qualification process
- Provide information to users and customers about the availability of services and the procedure for obtaining them
- Source and deliver the components of requested standard services
- Assist with general information, complaints or comments.

4.2 SCOPE (SO 4.3.2)

Some organizations deal with service requests through their incident management process (and tools), with service requests being handled as a particular type of 'incident'. However, there is a significant difference between an incident – usually an unplanned event – and a service request, which is something that should be planned. The process needed to fulfil a request varies depending upon exactly what is being requested, but it can usually be broken down into a set of activities that have to be performed.

Therefore, in an organization where large numbers of service requests have to be handled, and where the actions to be taken to fulfil those requests are very varied or specialized, it may be appropriate to handle service requests as a completely separate work stream. Ultimately it is up to each organization to decide and document which service requests it handles through the request fulfilment process and which have to go through other processes.

4.3   VALUE TO THE BUSINESS AND SERVICE LIFECYCLE (SO 4.3.3)

The value of request fulfilment includes:

- Quick and effective access to standard services; this can improve business productivity and/or quality
- A less bureaucratic system for requesting and receiving access to existing or new services, reducing the cost of providing these services
- Where fulfilment is centralized, having more control over services can reduce costs as supplier negotiation is also centralized and support costs are lower.

4.4   POLICIES, PRINCIPLES AND BASIC CONCEPTS (SO 4.3.4)

Examples of request fulfilment policies include:

- The request fulfilment activities follow a predefined process flow or model which includes all stages needed to fulfil the request, the individuals or support groups involved, target timescales and escalation paths

- The ownership of service requests resides with a centralized function; for example, the service desk, which monitors, escalates, despatches and may also fulfil the request
- Service requests that impact CIs are usually fulfilled by implementing a standard change
- All requests are logged, controlled, coordinated, promoted and managed via a single system
- All requests are authorized before activities are undertaken to fulfil them.

4.4.1 Request models

Service request models (which typically include one or more standard changes in order to complete fulfilment activities) are defined, to ensure that frequently used service requests are handled consistently and meet agreed service levels.

4.4.2 Menu selection

Request fulfilment offers great opportunities for self-help. Users are offered a self-help menu from which they can select requests and provide details.

4.4.3 Request status tracking

Track requests throughout their lifecycle to support proper handling of requests and reporting on their status. Within the request fulfilment system, status codes may be linked to requests to indicate where they are in relation to the lifecycle. Examples include: in review, suspended, awaiting authorization, rejected, cancelled, in progress, completed, and closed.

4.4.4   Financial approval

The cost of providing the service should first be established and submitted to the user for approval within their management chain. In some cases there may be a need for additional compliance approval, or wider business approval.

4.4.5   Coordination of fulfilment activities

Fulfilment activity depends upon the type of service request. Simple requests may be completed by the service desk, while others are forwarded to specialist groups and/or suppliers for fulfilment. The service desk monitors progress and keeps users informed throughout, regardless of the actual fulfilment source.

4.5   PROCESS ACTIVITIES, METHODS AND TECHNIQUES (SO 4.3.5)

4.5.1   Request receipt, logging and validation

Fulfilment work on service requests should not begin until a formalized request has been received, typically from the service desk. All service requests must be fully logged. Service request records include:

- Unique reference number
- Request categorization, urgency, impact and prioritization
- Date and time recorded, fulfilled and closed
- Name, ID, department and location of the person and/or group making the request
- Method of notification (for example, telephone, web interface, RFC, email, in person)
- Budget centre in case a charge is incurred
- Description of request

- Request status
- Related CIs
- Support group or person to which the service request is allocated.

4.5.2 Request categorization and prioritization

Requests can be categorized in several ways: for example, by service, activity, type, function or CI type.

Prioritization is determined by taking into account both the urgency of the request (how quickly the business needs to have it fulfilled) and the level of impact it is causing. The factors contributing to impact levels are as follows: the number of services impacted; the number of users or business units impacted; whether the requester is at an executive level; the level of financial gain or loss; the effect on business reputation; and regulatory or legislative requirements. A table can be generated for determining priority – Table 3.1 shows an example of a simple priority coding system.

There may also be occasions when, because of particular business expediency, normal priority levels have to be overridden. Some organizations may also recognize 'VIPs' whose service requests are handled as a higher priority than normal.

4.5.3 Request authorization

No work to fulfil a request should be done until it is authorized. Requests can be authorized via the service desk or by having pre-authorized requests. Alternatively, authorization may need to come from other sources; these could include access management, to determine whether the requester is authorized to make the request, or financial management, to authorize any charges or costs associated with fulfilling the request.

Service requests that cannot be authorized are returned to the requester with the reason for the rejection. The request record is also updated to indicate the rejection status.

4.5.4 Request review

The request is reviewed to determine the appropriate group to fulfil it. As requests are reviewed, escalated and acted upon, the request record is updated to reflect the current request status.

4.5.5 Request model execution

A request model documents a standard process flow, setting out the roles and responsibilities for fulfilling each request type to ensure that the fulfilment activities are repeatable and consistent. The relevant request model is chosen and executed for each service request.

Request models may be described as process steps and activities that are stored as reference documents in the service knowledge management system (SKMS). Alternatively they may be stored through specialized configurations within automated workflow tools or through code elements and configurations as part of web-based self-help solutions.

Any service requests that impact CIs in the live environment are authorized through change management, typically as standard changes.

4.5.6 Request closure

Fulfilled service requests are referred back to the service desk for closure. Having checked that the user is satisfied with the outcome, the service desk also ensures that any financial requirements are complete, confirms that the request categorization was correct (or if not, corrects it), carries out a user satisfaction survey, chases any outstanding documentation, and formally closes the request.

4.6 TRIGGERS, INPUTS, OUTPUTS AND INTERFACES (SO 4.3.6)

The trigger for request fulfilment is the user submitting a service request, either via the service desk or using a self-help facility. This often involves selection from a portfolio of available request types.

Inputs include:

- Work requests
- Authorization forms
- Service requests
- RFCs
- Requests from various sources such as phone calls, web interfaces or email
- Requests for information.

Outputs include:

- Authorized or rejected service requests
- Request fulfilment status reports
- Fulfilled service requests
- Incidents (rerouted)
- RFCs and standard changes
- Asset and CI updates
- Updated request records.

The primary interfaces are concerned with requesting services and their subsequent deployment:

- **Financial management for IT services** Interfaces may be needed if costs for fulfilling requests need to be reported and recovered
- **Service catalogue management** Links with request fulfilment to ensure that requests are well known to users and linked with services in the catalogue that they support
- **Release and deployment management** Some requests are for the deployment of new or upgraded components that can be automatically deployed
- **Service asset and configuration management** Once deployed, the configuration management system (CMS) has to be updated to reflect changes that may have been made as part of the fulfilment activities
- **Change management** Where a change is required to fulfil a request, it is logged as an RFC and progressed through change management
- **Incident and problem management** Requests may come in via the service desk and may initially be handled through the incident management process
- **Access management** Ensures that those making requests are authorized to do so in accordance with the information security policy.

4.7   INFORMATION MANAGEMENT (SO 4.3.7)

Request fulfilment is dependent on information from the following sources:

- **RFCs** The request fulfilment process may be initiated by an RFC, usually if the service request relates to a CI

- **Service portfolio** Enables the scope of agreed service requests to be identified
- **Security policies** Prescribe controls to be executed or adhered to, such as ensuring that the requester is authorized to access the service
- **Authorized approvers** People authorized to approve the requests.

Service requests contain information about which service is being asked for, who requested and authorized it, the process used to fulfil the request, the assignee and any actions, date and time of logging, and subsequent actions and closure details.

4.8   CRITICAL SUCCESS FACTORS AND KEY PERFORMANCE INDICATORS (SO 4.3.8)

The efficiency and effectiveness of the process can be measured by identifying critical success factors (CSFs) for the process, each CSF being supported by key performance indicators (KPIs):

- **CSF** Requests must be fulfilled in an efficient and timely manner that is aligned to agreed service level targets for each type of request:
    - **KPI** The mean elapsed time for handling each type of service request
    - **KPI** The number and percentage of service requests completed within agreed target times
    - **KPI** Breakdown of service requests at each stage (e.g. logged, work in progress, closed)
    - **KPI** Percentage of service requests closed by the service desk without reference to other levels of support (often referred to as 'first point of contact')

- **KPI** Number and percentage of service requests resolved remotely or through automation, without the need for a visit
- **KPI** Total numbers of requests (as a control measure)
- **KPI** The average cost per type of service request
- ■ **CSF** Only authorized requests are fulfilled:
  - **KPI** Percentage of service requests fulfilled that were appropriately authorized
  - **KPI** Number of incidents related to security threats from request fulfilment activities
- ■ **CSF** User satisfaction must be maintained:
  - **KPI** Level of user satisfaction with the handling of service requests (as measured in some form of satisfaction survey)
  - **KPI** Total number of incidents related to request fulfilment activities
  - **KPI** Size of the current backlog of outstanding service requests.

4.9   CHALLENGES AND RISKS (SO 4.3.9)

Challenges include:

- ■ Clearly defining the type of requests to be handled by the request fulfilment process
- ■ Establishing self-help capabilities at the front end that allow the users to interface successfully with the request fulfilment process
- ■ Agreeing and establishing service level targets
- ■ Agreeing the costs for fulfilling requests
- ■ Putting in place agreements for which services are standardized and who is authorized to request them

- Making information easily accessible about which requests are available
- Making requests follow a predefined standard fulfilment procedure
- The high impact of request fulfilment on user satisfaction.

Risks include:

- Poorly defined scope, where people are unclear about what the process is expected to handle
- Poorly designed or implemented user interfaces, meaning that users have difficulty raising requests
- Badly designed or operated back-end fulfilment processes that are incapable of dealing with the volume or nature of the requests
- Inadequate monitoring capabilities, meaning that accurate metrics cannot be gathered.

4.10 ROLES AND RESPONSIBILITIES (SO 6.7.7)

4.10.1 Request fulfilment process owner

Responsibilities include:

- Carrying out the generic process owner role for the request fulfilment process (see section 1.5)
- Designing request fulfilment models and workflows
- Working with other process owners to ensure there is an integrated approach across request fulfilment, incident management, event management, access management and problem management.

4.10.2 Request fulfilment process manager

Responsibilities include:

- Carrying out the generic process manager role for the request fulfilment process (see section 1.5)
- Planning and managing support for request fulfilment tools and processes, and coordinating interfaces with other service management processes
- Assisting with identification of suitable staffing levels to deliver request fulfilment activities and services
- Ensuring all authorized service requests are being fulfilled on a timely basis, in line with service level targets
- Representing request fulfilment activities at change advisory board (CAB) meetings
- Overseeing feedback from customers and reviewing request fulfilment activities for consistency, accuracy and effectiveness in order to proactively seek improvements.

4.10.3 Request fulfilment analyst

Responsibilities include:

- Providing a single point of contact and end-to-end responsibility to ensure submitted service requests have been processed
- Providing an initial triage of service requests to determine which IT resources will be engaged to fulfil them
- Communicating service requests to other IT resources that will be involved in fulfilling them
- Escalating service requests in line with established service level targets
- Ensuring service requests are appropriately logged.

5 Problem management

5.1 PURPOSE AND OBJECTIVES (SO 4.4.1)

The purpose of problem management is to manage problems through their lifecycle from first identification through investigation, documentation and eventual resolution and closure. Problem management seeks to minimize the adverse impact of incidents and problems on the business caused by underlying errors within the IT infrastructure, and to proactively prevent recurrence of incidents related to these errors.

The objectives of problem management are:

- To prevent problems and resulting incidents from happening
- To eliminate recurring incidents
- To minimize the impact of incidents that cannot be prevented.

5.2 SCOPE (SO 4.4.2)

Problem management includes diagnosing the root cause of incidents and determining the resolution of those problems. It is responsible for ensuring that the resolution is implemented through the appropriate control procedures, including change management and release and deployment management.

Problem management maintains information about problems and the appropriate workarounds and resolutions. This enables a reduction in the number and impact of incidents over time, with a strong interface to knowledge management and tools such as the known error database.

While incident and problem management are separate processes, they are closely related and typically use the same tools and similar categorization, impact and priority coding systems, ensuring effective communication when dealing with related incidents and problems.

A close relationship exists between proactive problem management activities and continual service improvement lifecycle activities that directly support identifying and implementing service improvements. Proactive problem management supports those activities through trending analysis and the targeting of preventive action. Identified problems from these activities become input to the continual service improvement register.

5.3   VALUE TO THE BUSINESS AND SERVICE LIFECYCLE (SO 4.4.3)

The value of problem management includes:

- Higher availability of IT services by reducing the number and duration of incidents
- Higher productivity of IT staff by reducing unplanned activity caused by incidents and resolving incidents more quickly through the use of recorded known errors and workarounds
- Reduction in the cost of fire-fighting effort or resolving repeat incidents.

5.4   POLICIES, PRINCIPLES AND BASIC CONCEPTS (SO 4.4.4)

Problem management policies include:

- Problems are tracked separately from incidents

- All problems are stored and managed in a single management system
- The classification of problems is standard across the enterprise.

5.4.1 Reactive and proactive problem management activities

Both reactive and proactive problem management activities raise problems, manage them through the problem management process, find the underlying causes of the incidents and prevent future recurrences of those incidents. The difference is in how the problem management process is triggered:

- **Reactive problem management** Triggered in reaction to an incident that has taken place, complementing incident management activities by focusing on the underlying cause of an incident to prevent its recurrence and identifying workarounds when necessary
- **Proactive problem management** Triggered by activities seeking to improve services, such as trend analysis activities, complementing continual service improvement activities by helping to identify workarounds and improvement actions that can improve the quality of a service.

5.4.2 Problem models

Many problems will be unique and require handling in an individual way. However, some incidents may recur because of dormant or underlying problems (for example, where the cost of a permanent resolution will be high and a decision has been taken not to go ahead with an expensive solution but to 'live with' the problem).

As well as creating a known error record in the known error database (KEDB) to ensure quicker diagnosis, a problem model can be created for handling such problems in the future.

5.4.3   Incidents versus problems

An incident is an unplanned interruption to an IT service or reduction in the quality of an IT service. A problem presents a different view of an incident by understanding its underlying cause. Incidents do not 'become' problems. While incident management activities are focused on restoring services to normal-state operations, problem management activities are focused on finding ways to prevent incidents from happening. It is quite common to have incidents that are also problems.

The rules for invoking problem management during an incident can vary at the discretion of individual organizations. Situations may include the following:

- Incident management cannot match an incident to existing problems and known errors
- Trend analysis of logged incidents reveals that an underlying problem might exist
- A major incident has occurred where problem management needs to identify the root cause
- An incident is resolved but no definitive cause has been identified and it is likely to recur
- Analysis of an incident reveals that an underlying problem exists, or is likely to exist.

5.4.4   Problem management techniques

There are many problem analysis, diagnosis and solving techniques available, including:

- **Chronological analysis** Documenting events in chronological order to provide a timeline of events
- **Pain value analysis** Analysing the level of pain caused to the organization or business by identified incidents and problems. A formula to calculate this pain level may include the number of people affected, duration of the downtime caused and cost to the business
- **Kepner and Tregoe** Formal problem analysis to investigate deeper-rooted problems in the following stages:
  - Defining the problem
  - Describing the problem in terms of identity, location, time and size
  - Establishing possible causes
  - Testing the most probable cause
  - Verifying the true cause
- **Brainstorming** Holding a meeting where people throw in ideas about the potential cause and suggest potential actions to resolve the problem
- **Five whys** Using the description of the event that took place and asking, 'Why did this occur?' Repeat until the fifth iteration, when typically the true root cause is found
- **Fault isolation** Re-executing the transactions or events that led to a problem step by step, one CI at a time, until the CI at fault is identified
- **Affinity mapping** Organizing large amounts of data into groupings based on common characteristics. Key concepts are identified and then grouped by similar traits. Each group is then examined for a potential root cause that may underlie them all

- **Hypothesis testing** Generating a list of possible root causes based on educated guesswork and then determining whether each hypothesis is true or false
- **Technical observation post** Bringing together specialist technical support staff to focus on a specific problem; monitoring events in real time to catch and identify the specific situation and establish the possible causes of the problem
- **Ishikawa diagrams** A method of documenting causes and effects where the main goal is represented by the trunk of the diagram, with primary factors represented as branches, secondary factors added as stems, and so on. The result is a 'fishbone' diagram
- **Pareto analysis** Separating the most important potential causes of failure from more trivial issues, on the basis of 80% of the value being derived from 20% of the effort.

5.4.5 Errors detected in the development environment

It is rare for any new applications, systems or software releases to be completely error-free. Often the more serious faults are resolved, but minor faults are not addressed. Where releases into the live environment include known deficiencies, these are logged as known errors in the KEDB, with details of workarounds or resolution activities.

5.5   PROCESS ACTIVITIES, METHODS AND TECHNIQUES (SO 4.4.5)

The problem management process flow for handling a recognized problem is shown in Figure 5.1.

Figure 5.1 Problem management process flow

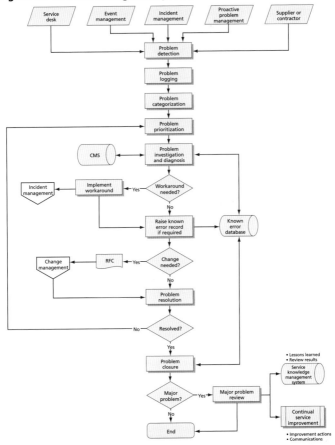

5.5.1 Problem detection

Problems may be detected in a number of ways:

- Suspicion of an unknown cause of one or more incidents
- The obvious existence of a major problem
- As a result of incident analysis
- Through the automated detection of a fault
- On notification of the existence of a problem by a supplier
- Through proactive problem management activities.

5.5.2 Problem logging

All relevant details of the problem are recorded and date- and/or time-stamped to allow control and escalation.

The problem record needs to be cross-referenced to the related incident records. The incident record is a good source of basic information for the problem record, and where the same tool is used for incident and problem management, this data may be transferred or linked automatically.

5.5.3 Problem categorization

The same categorization system must be used for problems as for incidents, enabling meaningful correlation between the two. Additionally, consistent categorization helps later with trend analysis activities and knowledge management – especially in the area of managing the KEDB. In many cases the category can be inherited from the associated incident record.

5.5.4 Problem prioritization

Problems must be prioritized in the same way as incidents. However, problem prioritization also takes into account the frequency and impact of the related incidents. Although individual incidents may have a low impact and urgency, if they occur frequently the cumulative effect may lead to a different prioritization of the related problem record.

Additionally, when determining the priority of a problem, the severity needs to be taken into account. Severity can be assessed by:

- The cost of recovering or replacing the impacted system
- The number of people and the types of skill required to solve the problem
- The length of time required to fix the problem
- The extent of the problem in terms of affected CIs.

5.5.5 Problem investigation and diagnosis

An investigation to diagnose the root cause is carried out. Appropriate levels of resource, skills and time need to be allocated based on the priority and category of the problem.

The configuration management system (CMS) is used to determine the extent, or potential extent, of the impact and can be useful in identifying the point of failure. It can be used to identify similar configurations against which to carry out further analysis.

It may be useful to attempt to recreate failure conditions in a test system that mirrors the live environment as far as possible.

5.5.6 Workarounds

A workaround is a temporary way of overcoming difficulties.

In some cases, before a root cause has been identified and resolved, it may be possible to put in place a workaround to resolve related incidents.

The problem record remains open while a workaround is in place.

5.5.7   Create a known error record

A known error record must be created whenever a root cause is known, and where a workaround is in place, and recorded in the KEDB. The KEDB holds records detailing previous incidents and problems, and how they were overcome. The KEDB is also used in the incident management process to determine whether the incident is related to a problem management record and, if there is a known workaround, to speed up the resolution of future related incidents.

It may be useful to create a known error record before the root cause is known or a workaround has been identified. In general a known error record should be created whenever it is useful to do so.

Take care to ensure the records in the KEDB are maintained so that they remain current and useful, and that duplicate records are minimized to avoid confusion.

5.5.8   Problem resolution

Once a solution has been identified, it needs to be applied as soon as possible. However, there may be constraints that delay resolution.

Resolution is usually managed as part of the change management process.

The costs or the disruption associated with making the necessary change may be prohibitive, so the decision may be taken to leave the problem record open and not apply the solution. This decision is recorded as part of the problem record.

5.5.9 Problem closure

When the resolution has been successfully applied, and the change completed, the problem record is closed along with any related open incident records. If there is a related known error record it is updated to show that the resolution has been applied.

As part of the closure activities a check is made on the completeness of all of the related records.

5.5.10 Major problem review

Following closure of a major problem, as determined by the organization's prioritization method, a review needs to be conducted to ensure lessons are learned for the future. This examines:

- What was done correctly
- What was done incorrectly
- What could be done better
- What could be done to prevent recurrence
- Any third-party responsibilities
- Whether follow-up actions are needed.

Where appropriate, output from the major problem review is shared with the customer to demonstrate that these events are being taken seriously and handled responsibly and consistently.

5.6   TRIGGERS, INPUTS, OUTPUTS AND INTERFACES (SO 4.4.6)

Triggers include:

- Reactive and proactive problem management, plus other problem records, and corresponding known error records

- One or more incidents via service desk staff or identified patterns and trends of incidents
- Supplier's notification of potential faults or known deficiencies
- Reviews of other sources such as operation or event logs, operation communications.

Inputs include:

- Incident records and incident reports for proactive problem trending
- Information about CIs and their status
- Communication about RFCs and releases
- Communication of events
- Operational and service level objectives
- Output from risk management and risk assessment activities.

Outputs include:

- Resolved problems and resolution actions, plus updated problem records
- RFCs
- Workarounds for incidents and known error records
- Problem management reports
- Output and improvement recommendations from major problem reviews.

Problem management provides a wealth of information and reports on the volumes and types of information to all other areas and processes. Interfaces include the following:

- **Financial management for IT services** Assists in assessing the impact of proposed resolutions or workarounds, as well as pain value analysis, with problem management providing management information about the cost of resolving and preventing problems, which is used as input into the budgeting and accounting systems and total cost of ownership calculations

- **Availability management** Uses proactive problem management to determine how to reduce downtime
- **Capacity management** Assists with the investigation of some problems (e.g. performance issues) and with assessing proactive measures. Problem management provides management information relative to the quality of decision-making during the capacity planning process
- **IT service continuity management (ITSCM)** Problem management acts as an entry point into ITSCM where a significant problem is not resolved before it starts to have a major impact on the business
- **Service level management (SLM)** Problem management contributes to improvements in service levels by analysing incidents and problems affecting the level of service, and its management information is used as the basis of SLA reviews. SLM also provides parameters within which problem management works, such as impact information and the effect on services of proposed resolutions and proactive measures
- **Change management** Involves problem management in rectifying the situation caused by failed changes. Problem management also ensures that all resolutions or workarounds that require a change to a CI are submitted through change management
- **Service asset and configuration management** Provides the CMS which assists problem management to identify faulty CIs and also to determine the impact of problems and resolutions
- **Release and deployment management** Is responsible for deploying problem fixes out into the live environment. It also helps in ensuring that the associated known errors are

transferred from development into the live KEDB. Problem management also helps to resolve problems caused by faults during the release process

- **Knowledge management** Provides the service knowledge management system (SKMS), which can be used to form the basis for the KEDB and record or integrate with the problem records

- **Seven-step improvement process** Incidents and problems provide a basis for identifying opportunities for service improvement and adding them to the continual service improvement register. Proactive problem management activities may also identify underlying problems and service issues that, if addressed, can contribute to increases in service quality and end-user or customer satisfaction.

5.7 INFORMATION MANAGEMENT (SO 4.4.7)

Problem management uses the following knowledge systems:

- **CMS** Holds the details of all of the components of the IT infrastructure, the relationships between these components as well as historical data on errors or faults. As such it plays a critical role supporting categorization, prioritization, and also in investigation and diagnosis activities

- **KEDB** To allow storage of previous knowledge of incidents and problems. The known error record details the fault, the symptoms and details of any workaround or resolution action. The KEDB should be used during incident and problem diagnosis to speed up the resolution process. The KEDB is part of the CMS and may be part of a larger SKMS.

5.8   CRITICAL SUCCESS FACTORS AND KEY PERFORMANCE INDICATORS (SO 4.4.8)

The efficiency and effectiveness of the process can be measured by identifying critical success factors (CSFs) for the process, each CSF being supported by key performance indicators (KPIs):

- **CSF** Minimize the impact to the business of incidents that cannot be prevented:
  - **KPI** The number of known errors added to the KEDB
  - **KPI** The percentage accuracy of the KEDB
  - **KPI** Percentage of incidents closed at 'first point of contact'
- **CSF** Maintain quality of IT services through elimination of recurring incidents:
  - **KPI** Total numbers of problems
  - **KPI** Size of current problem backlog for each IT service
  - **KPI** Number of repeat incidents for each IT service
- **CSF** Provide overall quality and professionalism of problem handling activities to maintain business confidence in IT capabilities:
  - **KPI** The number of major problems (opened and closed and backlog)
  - **KPI** The percentage of major problem reviews completed successfully and on time
  - **KPI** Number and percentage of problems incorrectly assigned or incorrectly categorized
  - **KPI** The backlog of outstanding problems and the trend
  - **KPI** Number and percentage of problems that exceeded their target resolution times
  - **KPI** Percentage of problems resolved and not resolved within SLA targets
  - **KPI** Average cost per problem.

Ideally, break down all metrics by category, impact, severity and urgency.

5.9   CHALLENGES AND RISKS (SO 4.4.9)

Challenges include:

- A major dependency for problem management is the establishment of an effective incident management process and tools
- The skills and capabilities of problem resolution staff to identify the true root cause of incidents
- The ability to relate incidents to problems can be a challenge if the tools used to record incidents are different from those of problems
- The ability to integrate problem management activities with the CMS to determine relationships between CIs and to refer to the history of CIs when performing problem support activities
- Ensuring that problem management is able to use all knowledge and service asset and configuration management resources available to investigate and resolve problems
- Ensuring that there is ongoing training of technical staff, both in technical aspects of their job and in the business implications of the services they support and the processes they use.

Risks include:

- Being inundated with problems that cannot be handled within acceptable timescales due to a lack of available or properly trained resources
- Becoming bogged down with problems, with the result that these problems are not solved as intended because there are inadequate support tools for investigation

■ Lack of adequate and/or timely information sources because of inadequate tools or lack of integration.

5.10   ROLES AND RESPONSIBILITIES (SO 6.7.6)

5.10.1 Problem management process owner

Responsibilities include:

■ Carrying out the generic process owner role for the problem management process (see section 1.5)
■ Designing incident models and workflows
■ Ensuring there is an integrated approach to incident management, problem management, event management, access management and request fulfilment.

5.10.2 Problem management process manager

Responsibilities include:

■ Carrying out the generic process manager role for the problem management process (see section 1.5)
■ Planning and managing support for problem management tools and processes, coordinating interfaces with other service management processes
■ Liaising with all problem resolution groups, suppliers, contractors etc. to ensure resolution of problems within SLA targets and contractual obligations
■ Ownership and maintenance of the KEDB
■ Formal closure of all problem records
■ Arranging, running and documenting major problem reviews and all related follow-up activities.

5.10.3 Problem analyst

Responsibilities include:

- Reviewing incident data and confirming correct prioritization and classification
- Investigating assigned problems through to resolution or root cause
- Coordinating others to assist with analysis and resolution actions for problems and known errors
- Raising RFCs to resolve problems
- Monitoring progress on the resolution of known errors and advising on available workarounds for incidents
- Updating the KEDB with new or updated known errors and workarounds
- Assisting with major incidents and identifying their root causes.

6   Access management

6.1   PURPOSE AND OBJECTIVES (SO 4.5.1)

Access management grants authorized users the right to use a service, or group of services, while preventing access to non-authorized users.

The objectives of access management are to:

- Manage access to services based on policies in information security management
- Respond efficiently to requests for granting, changing or restricting access rights; verifying whether requests are granted appropriately
- Oversee access to services and ensure that rights provided are not improperly used.

6.2   SCOPE (SO 4.5.2)

Access management is the execution of policies and actions defined in information security management, managing the confidentiality, availability and integrity of an organization's data and intellectual property.

Access management ensures the right of access but not availability of access, which is provided by availability management.

Access management can be initiated via a service request, but is executed by technical and application management functions, coordinated by the service desk or IT operations management.

6.3   VALUE TO THE BUSINESS AND SERVICE LIFECYCLE (SO 4.5.3)

Access management provides value by:

- Controlling access to services so that the organization effectively maintains the confidentiality of its information and achieves regulatory compliance (if required)
- Giving employees the appropriate access that they need in order to be effective
- Revoking access rights when needed
- Enabling the use of services to be audited, or abuse to be traced.

6.4   POLICIES, PRINCIPLES AND BASIC CONCEPTS (SO 4.5.4)

Examples of access management policies might include:

- Access management administration and activities are directed by the policies and controls in the information security policy
- Accesses to use services are logged and tracked, ensuring rights provided are appropriately used
- Access to services is maintained in alignment with changes in personnel events such as transfers and terminations
- An accurate history is maintained of who has accessed, or tried to access, services
- Procedures for handling, escalating and communicating security events are defined and aligned to the information security policy.

Access management enables users to access services documented in the service catalogue.

Key concepts include:

- **Access** The level and extent of a service's functionality or data that a user is entitled to use
- **Identity** Information that distinguishes each user and verifies his or her status in an organization; each identity is unique
- **Rights (or privileges)** Settings that enable a user to access a service in a particular way; for example, read, write, execute, change or delete
- **Service or service groups** As most users do not use just one service, and users with similar roles use a similar set of services, it is more efficient to grant each user or group of users access to a set of services in a group
- **Directory services** Tools used to manage access and rights.

6.5 PROCESS ACTIVITIES, METHODS AND TECHNIQUES (SO 4.5.5)

6.5.1 Requesting access

Access can be requested in a number of ways, including:

- Standard request generated by an HR system, such as for a new starter, promotion or leaver
- Request for change (RFC) or service request
- Execution of a pre-authorized script.

Rules for requesting access are usually documented in the service catalogue.

6.5.2   Verification

For every request, access management verifies that:

- The user requesting access is who they say they are. This type of verification depends on an organization's security policy; this is usually achieved by the user providing his or her username and password
- The user has a legitimate requirement for the service. This requires independent verification; for example:
  - Notification from HR or authorization from an appropriate manager
  - Submission of an RFC or service request, with supporting evidence, through change management
  - A policy stating the user is allowed access to an optional service if needed.

The RFC for new services specifies the users or user groups to be given access. Access management verifies that these users remain valid and then automatically provides access as specified in the RFC.

6.5.3   Providing rights

Access management does not decide who has which access rights; it executes the policies and regulations defined in service strategy and service design, enforcing decisions to restrict or provide access.

Following verification, the user is provided with the rights to use the requested service. Typically, this requires a request to action, which is sent to the relevant team supporting the service. Where possible, these actions should be automated.

Role conflict can occur where there are many roles and groups. It arises when two specific roles or groups, if assigned to a single user, create issues with separation of duties or conflicts of interest, such as:

- One role requires detailed access, while another prevents access
- Two roles allow a user to perform conflicting roles such as logging time and approving payment for that time.

Any conflict is documented and escalated for resolution.

For any role or group, there may be users who need something slightly different from the predefined role. Each exception is coordinated by access management and approved via the originating process.

Regular reviews of the roles and groups are performed to ensure that they remain appropriate, and unwanted or obsolete groups are removed.

6.5.4 Monitoring identity status

Users' roles and access needs change over time, for example, as a result of:

- Job changes, promotions, demotions or transfers
- Resignation, death or retirement
- Disciplinary actions or dismissals.

Access management documents the user lifecycle for each type of user and automates the process based on this.

Access management tools require facilities to change user states or move users between groups and maintain an audit trail.

6.5.5 Logging and tracking access

Access monitoring and control activities need to be included in the monitoring activities undertaken by technical and application management and all service operation processes.

Exceptions are handled by incident management. Specific incident models can be designed to handle abuse of access rights.

Information security management can use intrusion detection tools to detect unauthorized access and check what rights have been provided by access management.

Access management may be required to provide access records for forensic investigations. This is usually provided by operational staff, but working as part of the access management process.

6.5.6 Removing or restricting rights

Access management is responsible for revoking rights and executing the decisions and policies made during service strategy and service design.

Access is usually removed following a death, resignation, dismissal, role change or transfer.

Applying tighter restrictions, such as reducing levels, time or duration of access, should occur when a user changes roles, is demoted, is under investigation or is away on a temporary basis.

6.6   TRIGGERS, INPUTS, OUTPUTS AND INTERFACES (SO 4.5.6)

Access management can be triggered when access is requested, as detailed in section 6.5.1.

Inputs include:

- Information security policies
- Operational and service level requirements for granting access to services, performing access management administrative activities and responding to access management related events
- Authorized RFCs to access rights
- Authorized requests to grant or terminate access rights.

Outputs include:

- Provision of access to IT services
- Access records and history of access granted to services
- Access records and history where access has been denied and the reasons for the denial
- Timely communications concerning inappropriate access or abuse of services.

Interfaces include:

- **Demand management** Helps to identify the necessary resource levels to handle expected volumes of requests for access
- **Strategy management for IT services** It may be determined that some access management activities (especially for larger organizations) could be handled more efficiently within individual business organizations rather than in a centralized access management function
- **Information security management** Provides the security and data protection policies and tools needed to execute access management. Interfaces are also required with human resource processes to verify the user's identity to ensure they are entitled to the services being requested

- **Service catalogue management** Provides methods and means by which users can access different IT services, service descriptions and views that they are authorized for
- **IT service continuity management (ITSCM)** To manage access to services in the event of a major business disruption or in conditions where services have been temporarily sourced from alternative locations
- **Service level management (SLM)** Maintains the agreements for access to each service, including the criteria for who is entitled to access each service, the cost access and the level of access to be granted to different types of user
- **Change management** Controls the actual requests for access
- **Service asset and configuration management** To identify data storage and interrogate CIs to determine current access details
- **Request fulfilment** Provides methods and means by which users can request access to the standard services that are available to them.

6.7   INFORMATION MANAGEMENT (SO 4.5.7)

Access management holds unique information on the identity of each user. The details include:

- Name, address and contact details
- Physical documents, such as passport, driving licence
- A reference number, such as employee number
- Biometric information
- Expiry date, if relevant.

This data may relate to employees, contractors, vendor staff or customers (in the case of internet-based services). All data held about users is subject to data protection legislation and should be protected by each organization's security procedures.

Access management generates a username and password and has the information on the access types granted to the specific resources.

To be effective, access management needs the following information:

- Well-defined procedures between IT and HR that include fail-safe checks to ensure that access rights are removed as soon as they are no longer justified or required
- 'User profile', 'user template' or 'user role': used to describe the type of grouping for easier management of standard access
- The groups that users may belong to and the associated access requirements, although a user may have additional access requirements relating to their role. Some groups may have specific access requirements
- A catalogue of all the roles in the organization and which services support each role. This catalogue of roles is compiled and maintained by access management in conjunction with HR and may be automated in the directory services tools.

6.8 CRITICAL SUCCESS FACTORS AND KEY PERFORMANCE INDICATORS (SO 4.5.8)

The efficiency and effectiveness of the process can be measured by identifying critical success factors (CSFs) for the process, each CSF being supported by key performance indicators (KPIs):

- **CSF** Ensure that the confidentiality, integrity and availability of services are protected in accordance with the information security policy:
  - **KPI** Percentage of incidents that involved inappropriate security access or attempts at access to services

- **KPI** Number of audit findings that discovered incorrect access settings for users who have changed roles or left the company
- **KPI** Number of incidents requiring a reset of access rights
- **KPI** Number of incidents caused by incorrect access settings
- **CSF** Provide appropriate access to services on a timely basis to meet business needs:
    - **KPI** Percentage of requests for access (e.g. service request, RFC) that were provided within established service level agreements (SLAs) and operational level agreements (OLAs)
- **CSF** Provide timely communications about improper access or abuse of services on a timely basis:
    - **KPI** Average duration of access-related incidents (from time of discovery to escalation).

6.9   CHALLENGES AND RISKS (SO 4.5.9)

Challenges include:

- Monitoring and reporting on access activity as well as incidents and problems related to access
- Verifying the identity of a user, and that he or she qualifies for access to a specific service or the approving person or body
- Linking multiple access rights to an individual user
- Determining the status of users at any time
- Managing changes to a user's access requirements
- Restricting access rights to unauthorized users
- Building and maintaining a database of all users and the rights that they have been granted.

Risks include:

- Lack of appropriate supporting technologies to manage and control access to services, which can lead to a dependency on error-prone manual tasks
- Controlling access from 'back-door' sources such as application interfaces
- Managing and controlling access to services by external third-party suppliers
- Lack of management support for access management
- Access levels and management controls unnecessarily hindering the business.

6.10   ROLES AND RESPONSIBILITIES (SO 6.7.9)

6.10.1 Access management process owner

Responsibilities include:

- Carrying out the generic process owner role for the access management process (see section 1.5)
- Designing access request workflows
- Working with other process owners to ensure there is an integrated approach to the design and implementation of access management, incident management, event management, request fulfilment and problem management.

6.10.2 Access management process manager

Responsibilities include:

- Carrying out the generic process manager role for the access management process (see section 1.5)

- Planning and managing support for access management tools and processes
- Coordinating interfaces between access management and other service management processes.

6.10.3 Other access management roles

Responsibilities of service desk staff include:

- Providing a route to request access to a service via a service request. The service desk will validate the request, then pass it to the appropriate team to provide access. This team may have delegated responsibility for providing access for simple services during the call
- Communicating with the user when access has been granted and ensuring that he or she receives any other required support
- Detecting and reporting incidents related to access.

Responsibilities of technical and application management staff include:

- During service design, ensuring that mechanisms are created to simplify and control access management for each service; finding ways to detect and stop the abuse of rights
- During service transition, testing the service to ensure that access can be granted, controlled and prevented as designed
- During service operation, performing access management for the systems under their control and dealing with access-related incidents and problems
- Providing training to service desk or IT operations management to ensure that staff are adequately trained and that they have access to the appropriate tools to enable them to perform these tasks.

Responsibilities of IT operations management staff could include:

- Providing or revoking access to key systems or resources for each area
- Using the operations bridge to monitor events related to access management and provide first-line support and coordination in the resolution of those events where appropriate.

7 Service desk

7.1 ROLE (SO 6.3.1)

The service desk is the single point of contact for users when there is a service disruption. It can also be responsible for dealing with service requests and for some categories of request for change (RFC).

The service desk plays a critical role in the delivery of services by providing:

- Improved customer service, perception and satisfaction
- Increased accessibility through a single point of contact, communication and information
- Better quality and faster turnaround of customer or user requests
- Improved teamwork and communication
- Enhanced focus and a proactive approach to service provision
- Reduced negative business impact
- Better-managed infrastructure and control
- Improved usage of IT support resources and increased productivity of business personnel
- More meaningful management information for decision support.

The service desk commonly acts as an 'entry level' function for IT staff. Working on the service desk provides excellent first-line experience for anyone wishing to pursue a career in service management.

7.2 OBJECTIVES (SO 6.3.2)

The primary aim of the service desk is to provide a single point of contact between the services being provided and the users.

A typical service desk:

- Manages incidents and service requests
- Handles communication with the users
- Executes the incident management and request fulfilment processes to restore the normal-state service operation to the users as quickly as possible. ('Restoration of service' is meant in the widest possible sense, such as fixing a technical fault, fulfilling a service request or answering a query; whatever is needed to allow the users to return to working satisfactorily.)

Specific responsibilities include:

- Logging all relevant incident and service request details and allocating categorization and prioritization codes
- Providing first-line investigation and diagnosis
- Resolving incidents and service requests at this level if possible
- Escalating incidents and service requests where they cannot be resolved within agreed timescales
- Keeping users informed of progress
- Closing all resolved incidents and service requests
- Conducting customer satisfaction surveys
- Maintaining communication with users:
  - Keeping users informed of incident progress
  - Notifying users of impending changes or agreed outages.

7.3   ORGANIZATIONAL STRUCTURES (SO 6.3.3)

7.3.1   Local service desk

A local service desk is located close to or within the user community it serves, aiding communications and providing a visible presence. However, it can be expensive and inefficient to resource.

Reasons to maintain a local desk include:

- Language and cultural or political differences
- Different time zones
- Specialized groups of users
- Customized or specialized services that require specialist knowledge
- VIP or criticality status of users.

7.3.2   Centralized service desk

In this arrangement, the service desk function is centrally located. It may consolidate a number of local service desks into a single location or a smaller number of locations. This can be more efficient and cost-effective, as fewer staff are required to deal with a higher volume of calls; these staff have greater skill levels because there is a higher frequency of events. Some form of local presence might still be necessary to handle physical support requirements, although these would be controlled from the central desk.

7.3.3   Virtual service desk

A virtual service desk uses technology to give the impression of a single centralized service desk, although it may be staffed by personnel in different locations or functional areas of the organization. This approach gives the options of home working, secondary support groups, offshoring or outsourcing to meet user demand. However, if the virtual service desk model is used, it is important to ensure consistency of service quality, terms and common processes and tools.

7.3.4   Follow the sun

An organization using the 'follow-the-sun' model combines two or more geographically dispersed service desk functions, each typically operating in 'normal working hours', to provide a 24-hour service for all users at relatively low cost. However, under this option it is important to ensure consistency of service quality, terms and common processes and tools.

7.3.5   Specialized service desk groups

In some circumstances it may be effective to create specialized service desk groups. These may be based on:

- VIP customers
- Business processes
- Culture or language.

Technology can be employed to capture the caller requirements and to route calls to the specialist group as appropriate. This can accelerate restoration of normal service for the groups served.

7.3.6   Building a single point of contact

Regardless of the model chosen for the service desk function, it is important to ensure that individual users are in no doubt as to whom they should contact if they need assistance.

The service desk needs to be seen as the single point of contact for the user, so it is advisable to ensure that there is just one telephone number, one user help portal and one email address to use in all cases.

These contact details need to be adequately advertised. This may be done in a number of ways: for example, by including the contact details on CI labels; setting up speed-dial buttons on telephones; distributing a corporate screen saver which displays service desk contacts; or printing the details on give-away items such as pens, mouse mats and coasters.

Ensure the details are prominent on business cards, correspondence and notice boards.

7.4 STAFFING OPTIONS (SO 6.3.4)

7.4.1 Staffing levels

When designing and staffing the service desk, an organization must provide the correct number of appropriately trained staff to respond to the level of demand and to maintain committed levels of service.

Organizations are usually faced with a challenge when doing this. Levels of demand for the service desk vary, based on a number of factors:

- **Demand levels on the business itself** Higher levels of business may be experienced at certain times of the year or at specific points in a month. When designing and staffing a service desk the service provider must take steps to understand these fluctuations in business demand

■ **Release and deployment of new IT services** When changes are introduced into the IT infrastructure, calls to the service desk may increase. These may be due to problems with the new functionality or a lack of training in how to use the service. Additionally, a new service may result in more service requests being made to the service desk from users wishing to use the new service.

Many organizations experience increased call rates during the start of the business day and again after lunch. Staffing a service desk to deal with these peaks can lead to inefficiency at other times when there are more service desk staff available than is necessary to meet the demand.

Consider the following factors when determining staffing levels:

■ Customer service expectations
■ Business requirements such as available budget and call and resolution response times
■ Size, age, design and complexity of the IT infrastructure
■ Number of customers and users to support, plus associated factors:
  – User skill levels
  – Language requirements
■ Incident and service request types and the implications for the amount of time needed to respond, the different volumes expected and the internal expertise required to address the requests
■ Period of support cover required, which can be influenced by a number of factors:
  – Hours covered
  – Out-of-hours support requirements
  – Time zones covered

- Locations to be supported, especially if desk-side support is required
- Workload patterns
- Agreed service level targets
- Type of response required (email, telephone, in person)
- Level of training required (and the ongoing training requirements)
- Support technologies available
- Existing staff skill levels
- Processes and procedures in use.

Tools are available to assist with workload modelling, which can help to determine optimum staffing levels. However, in order to produce meaningful results, these tools are dependent on detailed understanding of the above factors and having accurate data.

7.4.2   Skill levels

The organization must decide on the level and range of skills it requires to fulfil the requirements of the service desk. There is a range of possible skill options, from simple call logging through to detailed technical understanding. In most cases the service desk employs a combination of skills somewhere along that scale.

A skills base that is closer to the 'call-logging' end of the scale results in high call handling but lower service desk resolution rates. Moving to the other end of the scale increases resolution rates but decreases call-handling rates. An organization must determine the best point on the scale to deliver the service as required by the customer and detailed in service level targets.

Generally, higher targets result in higher costs to meet those targets.

Where there is a requirement to balance high service targets and the available budget, the optimum and most cost-effective approach is generally to implement a service desk that provides high-quality call-logging functionality, is focused on resolving the simpler requests and is highly efficient in identifying and implementing appropriate escalation to second- and third-line support where necessary.

If this is backed up by effective problem management and knowledge management processes, over time the service desk can resolve more and more calls, thereby improving quality and customer perception.

This can also be achieved by co-locating more technically skilled second-line support staff with the service desk, so more calls are resolved. Another advantage is that the second-line staff can be on hand to provide advice and additional training to the first-line service desk staff. This can require greater management control of the function and the need to ensure that other duties of the second-line staff do not suffer, such as in carrying out problem management activities. It is also possible that inappropriate emphasis may be placed on faster resolution of incidents, when a better, long-term result may be to focus on removing the root cause of the incidents.

Another factor influencing the number of staff and the level of skills required on the service desk is the level of customization or specialization of the supported applications. Generally, the more standardized the solution, the less it requires specialized skills to support it.

7.4.3 Training

Once the skills requirements are understood a formal training programme can be put in place and maintained. This ensures that the required skills can be provided and subsequently maintained and enhanced. Training covers:

- Interpersonal skills
- Business awareness
- Service awareness
- Technical awareness
- Diagnostic skills and techniques
- Supporting tools
- Process awareness
- The importance of data quality.

To be effective, the service desk skill levels and requirements need to be reassessed periodically and accurate training records maintained.

Shadowing and mentoring can be effective training methods for the service desk function. Shadowing involves experienced staff working alongside new staff or staff taking on new responsibilities in order to pass on knowledge and experience. This may start with the expert taking calls and the trainee listening in so they can learn how to deal with the users and respond to different types of request. Gradually, the trainee deals with more and more of the calls on their own. Eventually the expert takes the role of a mentor to the trainee, providing assistance only on request and at regularly planned review sessions.

The organization must plan to provide training to the staff who shadow and/or mentor their colleagues on the service desk.

The organization must be careful not to rely entirely on coaching and mentoring by internal staff, but also to maintain a commitment to a wider, formalized programme of staff development. This improves motivation and career planning, and ensures that the function is regularly exposed to external approaches and developments in providing service desk support. There is a risk, with a purely internal training programme, of missing out on new developments and of rewarding and reinforcing potentially negative approaches and activities.

7.4.4 Staff retention

It is vital that senior management recognizes the importance of the service desk and, consequently, the high value of the staff who work on it. A good service desk can suffer enormously from a significant loss of staff, so efforts need to be made to ensure it remains an attractive place to work.

This can be done in various ways:

- Proper recognition of the role and its importance to the organization
- Adequate and properly designed reward packages
- Team-building exercises
- Staff rotation to other activities (e.g. projects, second-line support).

The service desk can be a route to other functions in the organization or into supervisory or managerial roles. Take care to properly define and develop internal career paths and opportunities, and to ensure that appropriate succession planning is in place to enable career progression to take place without negatively affecting service delivery.

7.4.5 Super users

Many organizations find it useful to appoint or designate a number of super users throughout the user community to act as liaison points with IT in general and with the service desk in particular. They can:

■ Be used as a communication channel between the user and the IT community

■ Filter requests and incidents raised by the user community

■ Carry out the initial logging, categorization and prioritization of calls

■ Train user staff in new services and the service providers' processes and tools.

Where a super user's role is to screen and log calls, ensure that all relevant data is captured relating to the calls that they deal with, and not just those logged, for passing to IT. This provides valuable management information and, if not done correctly, can hide underlying problems from the IT organization.

Super users do not necessarily provide support for the whole of IT. In most cases they provide support for a specific application, module or business area.

Where super users form part of the service desk function they must be included in the service desk training and awareness programme and take part in any additional service desk team-building activities. This ensures that they remain effective in their contribution and have a strong sense of being part of the service desk team.

7.5 MEASURING SERVICE DESK PERFORMANCE (SO 6.3.5)

Metrics need to be established so that performance of the service desk can be evaluated at regular intervals, assessing the health, maturity, efficiency and effectiveness of the function, and identifying any opportunities to improve service desk operations.

Service desk metrics must be carefully chosen to ensure that they are realistic and that they accurately reflect performance. In some cases, simple metrics that are assumed to show a certain type of performance may be chosen. However, those assumptions may be incorrect; for example, the total number of calls to the service desk is not, in itself, an indicator of good or bad performance.

Metrics need to be used in conjunction with other measures and management information to determine the reasons for any increase or decrease in calls. It is useful to be able to compare this against the customer's perception of the service, which can be gathered using a customer satisfaction survey, as described in section 7.5.1.

Some examples of useful service desk metrics, to be collected and analysed for trends over time, include:

- First-line resolution rate showing the percentage of calls resolved by the service desk function, broken down by:
    - Percentage of calls resolved during the first contact with the user
    - Percentage resolved by the service desk staff alone compared to the percentage resolved by the first-line service desk staff and second-line support staff combined
- Average time to escalate an incident when first-line resolution is not possible

- Average service desk cost of handling an incident, which can be reported in different ways; for example:
  - Total cost of the service desk divided by the number of calls, giving basic high-level planning indications
  - Total cost of the service desk divided by the total call duration time, calculating the cost for individual calls, which can be combined with categorization data to allow more detailed and specific analysis to be carried out
- Percentage of user updates conducted within target times
- Average time to review and close a resolved call
- Number of calls broken down by time of day and day of the week, combined with the average call-time metric; this is critical to determining staff level requirements.

7.5.1 Customer satisfaction surveys

It is important that the service desk maintains data on customer perception of the service. Customer satisfaction is a critical success factor (CSF) for the service desk. Aspects for a survey to focus on include:

- How well the customers feel their calls have been answered
- Whether the service desk agent was courteous
- Whether the agent instilled confidence in the user.

A number of survey techniques and tools are available:

- **After-call survey** Callers are asked to remain on the line after the call and asked to rate the service
- **Outbound telephone survey** Customers who have used the service desk are contacted some time after their experience

- **Personal interviews** Customers are interviewed individually by the person carrying out the survey; this is especially useful for customers who use the service extensively or who feel they have had a particularly bad experience
- **Group interviews** Customers are interviewed in small groups to gather general impressions of the service
- **Postal or email surveys** Survey questionnaires are mailed to a target set of customers for their responses
- **Online surveys** Questionnaires are available on a website and customers are invited to participate.

It is advisable to keep the number of questions to a minimum and, where possible, align them to the specific customer experience.

To allow adequate comparison, the same percentage of calls should be selected in each period and calls rigorously carried out, despite any other time pressures.

7.6 OUTSOURCING THE SERVICE DESK (SO 6.3.6)

If the decision is made to outsource the service desk function, it is vital that the organization retains responsibility for the activities and the services provided.

There are a number of areas to consider to safeguard the service:

- Common tools and processes should be shared by the two organizations to allow a smooth processing flow. The outsourced service desk should have access to:
  - All incident records and information
  - Problem records and information
  - Known error records
  - Change schedule

- Sources of internal knowledge, especially second- and third-line support
- Configuration management system (CMS)
- Alerts from monitoring tools

■ Service level agreements (SLAs) for incident handling and resolution must be agreed by all parties and reflected in operational level agreements (OLAs) and underpinning contracts (UCs)

■ Good lines of communication need to be maintained between the outsourced service desk and the organization's other support teams. This can be assisted by some or all of the following steps:
- Close physical co-location
- Regular liaison and review meetings
- Cross-training tutorials between the teams and departments
- Partnership arrangements, where staff from both organizations are used jointly to staff the service desk

■ Ownership of data:
- Data collected by the outsourced service desk needs to be agreed and detailed in the underpinning contract with the outsource provider
- Data relative to the users, customers, CIs, services, incidents, service requests, changes etc. needs to remain with the organization that is outsourcing the service desk
- Data specifically related to the performance of the outsourcing provider's employees must remain under the ownership of that company. This may also apply to other data that is relevant only for the internal management of the outsourcing company.

8   Service operation functions

8.1   FUNCTIONS

A function is a logical concept that refers to the people and automated measures that execute a defined process, an activity or a combination of processes or activities. The service operation functions are needed to manage the 'steady state' operational IT environment.

The service desk function is described in Chapter 7.

Technical and application management can be organized in any combination and number of departments. The second-level groupings in Figure 8.1 are examples of typical groups of activities performed by technical management and are not a suggested organizational structure.

IT operations management may be a single central organization, or some activities and staff that may be provided by distributed or specialized departments (as illustrated in Figure 8.1) by overlapping with technical and application management functions.

8.2   TECHNICAL MANAGEMENT

Technical management provides detailed technical skills and resources to support the ongoing operation of the IT infrastructure. It also plays an important role in the design, testing, release and improvement of IT services. It refers to the groups, departments and teams that provide technical expertise and overall management of the IT infrastructure.

Figure 8.1 Service operation functions

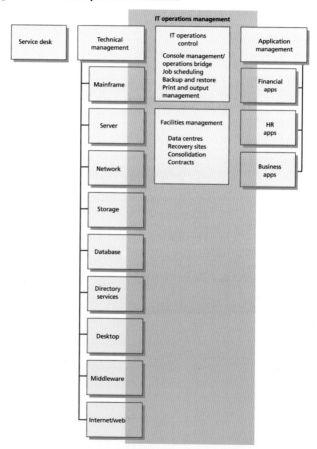

8.2.1 Role (SO 6.4.1)

Technical management fulfils a dual role:

■ Responsible for the technical knowledge and expertise relating to the management of the IT infrastructure, ensuring the knowledge required to design, build, transition, operate and improve the technology is identified, developed and refined
■ Providing the resources required to support the ITSM lifecycle, ensuring the technical resources are effectively trained and deployed to design, build, transition, operate and improve the technology.

By performing these two roles, technical management ensures that the organization has access to the right level of human resources to manage the technology and that there is the correct balance between the skill level, utilization and cost of these resources. This is especially true with regard to expensive specialist staff required for tactical, project and problem resolution activities. For larger organizations, specialist staff can be shared from central pools so that they are well utilized, provide economy of scale to the organization and minimize the need to hire contractors.

Technical management also provides guidance to IT operations on how best to carry out the ongoing operational management of technology. This is carried out partly during the service design process, and also through day-to-day communications with IT operations management.

8.2.2 Objectives (SO 6.4.2)

The objectives of technical management are to help plan, implement and maintain a stable infrastructure supporting the organization's business processes through:

- Well-designed, highly resilient and cost-effective infrastructure
- The use of technical skills to maintain the technical infrastructure in optimum condition
- The use of technical skills to speedily diagnose and resolve any technical failures.

8.2.3 Activities (SO 6.4.3)

There are two types of activity that technical management is involved in:

- Activities that are generic to the technical management function as a whole, discussed in this section
- A set of discrete activities and processes, which are performed by all three functions of technical, application and IT operations management (covered in section 8.3.3), plus technology management activities such as mainframe, server, middleware, network, desktop, internet, storage or archive, database and directory services management.

The key technical management activities include:

- Identifying the knowledge and expertise required, the skills that exist in the organization as well as those skills that need to be developed, and initiating training programmes to develop and refine the appropriate skills
- Participating in the definition of standards and technology architectures, the design and creation of new services to meet the standards required, and taking part in enhancement and operational projects
- Assisting with risk assessment, identifying critical services and system dependencies and defining and implementing countermeasures

- Designing and performing tests for the functionality, performance and manageability of IT services
- Managing vendors and contracts
- Defining and managing event management standards and tools, and also monitoring and responding to many categories of events
- Assisting incident and problem management
- Assisting with evaluation and building of changes and the deployment of releases
- Assisting continual service improvement processes in identifying opportunities for improvement and evaluating alternative solutions
- Defining and assisting with the operational activities performed as part of IT operations management.

8.3   IT OPERATIONS MANAGEMENT

IT operations management is the function responsible for the ongoing management and maintenance of an organization's IT infrastructure to ensure delivery of the agreed level of service to the business.

8.3.1   Role (SO 6.5.1)

IT operations management has two main areas of responsibility:

- Performing the activities and meeting the performance standards defined during service design and tested during service transition. The primary role of IT operations management is to maintain a stable infrastructure and consistency of IT service

■ Supporting the ability of the business to meet its objectives; this depends on the output and reliability of the day-to-day IT operations. IT operations adds value to the business as a part of the overall value network.

IT operations must maintain a balance between these activities and roles. This requires:

■ An understanding among all staff of how technology and technology performance affect the delivery of IT services
■ An understanding of the relative importance and impact of the services
■ Processes, procedures and manuals
■ A clearly defined set of achievement metrics for reporting
■ A cost strategy for balancing the requirements of different business units with cost savings through the optimization of technology
■ A value-based strategy for return on investment rather than a cost-based one.

8.3.2 Objectives (SO 6.5.2)

The objectives of IT operations management include:

■ Maintenance of the status quo to ensure that the organization's day-to-day processes and activities are stable
■ Regular monitoring and improvement to achieve higher-quality service at reduced costs, while maintaining stability
■ Rapid application of operational skills to diagnose and resolve IT operation failures.

8.3.3   Activities (SO 6.5.3)

Some technical and applications management groups or teams manage and execute their own operational activities, whereas others delegate these activities to a dedicated IT operations function.

The main activities involved within IT operations are:

- **Operations control** Oversees the execution and management of the IT infrastructure operational events and activities. This can be accomplished using an operations bridge or network operations centre. As well as performing routine tasks, operations control also performs specific tasks:
  - **Console management** Defining central observation and monitoring capability, then using the consoles for monitoring and control activities
  - **Job scheduling** Management of routine batch jobs, scripts and schedules
  - **Backup and restore** On behalf of all users, customers, teams and technology
  - **Print and output management** For the collation and distribution of all centralized printing and electronic output
  - **Maintenance activities** On behalf of all teams and departments
- **Facilities management** Manages the physical environments, data centre, computer rooms and recovery sites, including all power and cooling equipment.

8.4 APPLICATION MANAGEMENT

Application management is responsible for managing applications throughout their lifecycle. This function supports and maintains operational applications and also plays an important role in the design, testing and improvement of applications that form part of IT services.

8.4.1 Role (SO 6.6.1)

Application management is to applications what technical management is to the IT infrastructure. It plays a role in all applications, whether purchased or developed in-house. It contributes to the key decision on whether to buy an application or to build it (covered in *ITIL Service Design*, Chapter 3).

Once this decision has been made, application management plays a dual role:

- Custodian of technical knowledge and expertise related to managing applications, ensuring that the knowledge required to design, test, manage and improve IT services is identified, developed and refined
- Provider of the resources to support the ITSM lifecycle, ensuring that resources are effectively trained and deployed to design, build, transition, operate and improve the technology required to deliver and support IT services.

By performing these two roles, application management is able to ensure that the organization has access to the correct type and level of human resources to manage applications and so meet business objectives. Application management is also responsible for maintaining a balance between the skill level and the cost of these resources.

In addition to these two high-level roles, application management also performs the following specific roles:

■ Providing guidance to IT operations about how best to carry out the ongoing operational management of applications. This role is partly carried out during the service design process, but also through day-to-day communications with IT operations management

■ Integrating the application management lifecycle into the ITSM lifecycle. The objectives and activities that enable application management to play these roles effectively are outlined in sections 8.4.2 and 8.4.3.

8.4.2 Objectives (SO 6.6.2)

The objectives of application management are to:

■ Support the organization's business processes by helping identify functional and manageability requirements for application software

■ Assist in the design and deployment of applications and the ongoing support and improvement of those applications.

These objectives are achieved through:

■ Applications that are well-designed, resilient and cost-effective

■ Ensuring that the necessary functionality is available to achieve the required business outcomes

■ Organization of adequate technical skills to maintain operational applications in optimum condition

■ Swift use of technical skills to rapidly diagnose and resolve any technical failures that do occur.

8.4.3 Activities (SO 6.6.5)

Most application management teams or departments are dedicated to specific applications or sets of applications, but undertake some common activities including:

- Identifying the knowledge and expertise required to manage and operate applications in the delivery of IT services, and initiating training programmes to develop and refine the skills
- Designing and delivering end-user training, either by application development or application management groups, or by a third party. Application management is responsible for ensuring that training is conducted as appropriate
- Defining standards for the design of new architectures, participating in the design and building of new services, contributing to the design of the technical architecture and performance standards for IT services
- Designing and performing tests for the functionality, performance and manageability of IT services, designing applications to meet the levels of service required by the business, including modelling and workload forecasting
- Assisting in risk assessment, identifying critical service and system dependencies and defining and implementing countermeasures
- Managing suppliers of specific applications within the service level management and supplier management processes
- Participating in definition of event management standards and the instrumentation of applications for the generation of meaningful events
- Supporting problem management in validating and maintaining the known error database (KEDB) with application development teams

■ Evaluating changes (many changes are built by application management teams) and driving release management for their applications

■ Participating in defining the operational activities performed as part of IT operations management. Application management may perform the operational activities as part of an organization's IT operations management function.

Application management teams or departments are needed for all key applications. The role varies depending on the applications being supported, but generic responsibilities include:

■ Third-level support for incidents related to the application

■ Involvement in operation-testing plans and deployment issues

■ Application bug tracking and patch management (coding fixes for in-house code, transports and/or patches for third-party code)

■ Involvement in application operability and supportability issues such as error code design, error messaging, event management hooks

■ Application sizing and performance; volumetrics and load testing etc. in support of capacity and availability management processes

■ Involvement in developing release policies

■ Identification of enhancements to existing software, for both functionality and manageability.

9 Technology and implementation

9.1 GENERIC REQUIREMENTS FOR IT SERVICE MANAGEMENT TECHNOLOGY (SO 7.1)

The same technology should be used at all stages of the service lifecycle. Generally this includes:

- **Self-help** A web front end offering a menu-driven range of self-help and service requests. It should have a direct interface with the process-handling software at the back end
- **Workflow or process engine** To allow predefinition and control of defined processes such as incident lifecycle, request fulfilment lifecycle and change models. It should allow predefinition and management of responsibilities, activities, timescales, escalation paths and alerting
- **Integrated configuration management system (CMS)** To manage information about all the organization's IT infrastructure and other CIs, together with required attributes and relationships. It should support links, for example, to incidents, problems, known errors, change records and release records
- **Discovery, deployment and licensing technology** To populate or verify CMS data and assist in licence management. It can often also be used to deploy software, ideally with an interface to self-help
- **Remote control** To enable support personnel to take control of users' desktops to conduct investigations or correct settings. It must include appropriate security controls

- **Diagnostic utilities** Including scripts and case-based reasoning tools. Ideally it should present automated context-sensitive scripts
- **Reporting** Tools should include good reporting capabilities and a means for providing data to industry-standard reporting packages and dashboards
- **Dashboards** To provide 'at a glance' visibility of overall IT service performance. Displays can also be included in management reports. Dynamic, customized web-based views can be very useful
- **Integration with business service management** To allow combined views of ITSM and business-related IT.

9.2 EVALUATION CRITERIA FOR TECHNOLOGY AND TOOLS (SD 7.2)

Some generic points that organizations should consider when selecting any service management tool include:

- Data handling, integration, import, export and conversion
- Data backup, control and security
- Ability to integrate multi-vendor components, existing and into the future
- Conformity with international open standards
- Usability, scalability and flexibility of implementation and usage
- Support options provided by the vendor, and credibility of the vendor and tool
- The platform the tool will run on and how this fits the IT strategy
- Training and other requirements for customizing, deploying and using the tool
- Costs: initial and ongoing.

It is generally best to select a fully integrated tool, but this must support the processes used by the organization, and extensive tool customization should be avoided.

Consideration should also be given to the organization's exact requirements. These should be documented in a statement of requirements. Tool requirements should be categorized using MoSCoW analysis:

- M – MUST have this
- S – SHOULD have this if at all possible
- C – COULD have this if it does not affect anything else
- W – WON'T have this, but WOULD like in the future.

Each proposed tool can be evaluated against these criteria to ensure that the most appropriate option is selected.

9.3   EVALUATION CRITERIA FOR TECHNOLOGY AND TOOLS FOR PROCESS IMPLEMENTATION

9.3.1   Event management (SO 7.2)

Event management technology should have the following features:

- A multi-environmental, open interface to:
    - Allow monitoring and alerting across heterogeneous services and the entire IT infrastructure
    - Accept any standard (e.g. simple network management protocol) event input and generation of multiple alerting
- 'Standard' agents to monitor the most common environments, components and systems
- Configurable and programmable functionality to support correlation, assessment and handling of alerts, manipulation and routing of events (centralized or local)

- Capability to suppress or flag events during periods of scheduled outages
- Capability to allow an operator to acknowledge an alert, and if no response is entered within a defined timeframe, to escalate the alert
- Good reporting functionality.

Technology should allow a direct interface into the organization's incident management and escalation processes to support staff, third-party suppliers and engineers.

9.3.2 Incident management (SO 7.3)

Integrated ITSM technology should have the following features:

- Incident-logging capabilities that allow for efficient entry of incident data, categorization, prioritization, tracking and reporting of incidents
- An integral CMS to allow automated relationships to be made and maintained and used to assist in prioritization, investigation and diagnosis
- A process flow engine to allow processes to be predefined and automatically controlled
- Automated alerting and escalation capabilities
- A web interface to allow self-help and service requests to be input via internet or intranet screens
- An integrated known error database (KEDB)
- Easy-to-use reporting facilities
- Diagnostic tools.

Note that target times should be included in the support tools that are used to automate the workflow control and escalation paths.

9.3.3 Request fulfilment (SO 7.4)

Integrated ITSM technology is needed so that service requests can be linked to related incidents or events.

Some organizations may use the incident management element of ITSM tools and treat service requests as a subset and defined category of incidents. Request fulfilment technology should have the following capabilities:

- **Front-end self-help capabilities** To allow users to submit requests via some form of web-based, menu-driven selection process which may be integrated with an IT service catalogue and access controls to validate service requesters prior to fulfilment
- **Workflow engine capabilities** To automate work steps and authorization tasks for supporting service request models and fulfilment activities.

Otherwise the facilities required are very similar to those for managing incidents and changes: for example, predefined workflow control of models, priority levels, automated escalation and effective reporting.

9.3.4 Problem management (SO 7.5)

Problem management should have the following features:

- An integrated ITSM tool that differentiates between incidents and problems
- Integration with change management. This is very important, so that request, event, incident and problem records can be related to the requests for change (RFCs) that have caused problems

■ Integration with the CMS. This is needed to allow problem
   records to be linked to the components affected and the
   services. Service asset and configuration management forms
   part of a larger service knowledge management system (SKMS)
   which includes linkages to many of the data repositories used
   in service operation
■ An effective KEDB. This is an essential requirement to allow
   easy storage and retrieval of known error data
■ Good reporting facilities.

Note that in some cases the components or systems that are
being investigated by problem management may have been
provided by third-party vendors or manufacturers. Therefore,
vendors' support tools and/or KEDBs may also need to be used.

9.3.5 Access management (SO 7.6)

Access management uses a variety of technologies, including:

■ Human resource management technology, to authenticate the
   identity of users, authorize their access, and track their status
■ Directory services technology to enable technology managers
   to assign names to resources on a network and then provide
   access to those resources based on the profile of the user.
   Directory services tools also enable access management to
   create roles and groups and to link these to both users
   and resources
■ Access management features in applications, middleware,
   operating systems and network operating systems
■ Change management systems
■ Request fulfilment technology.

9.3.6 Service desk (SO 7.7)

Telephony systems used by the service desk should include:

- An automatic call distribution system to allow group pick-up capabilities from a single telephone number
- Computer telephony integration software to allow caller recognition and the incident record from the CMS to be automatically updated with the user's details
- Voice-over internet protocol, which can reduce telephony costs
- Statistical software to allow telephony statistics to be gathered and analysed:
  - Number of calls received, in total and broken down by any 'splits'
  - Call arrival profiles and answer times
  - Call abandon rates
  - Call handling rates by individual service desk call handlers
  - Average call durations
- Hands-free headsets, with dual-user access capabilities for use, for example, during training of new staff.

The following support tools will be particularly beneficial for use by the service desk:

- An integrated KEDB to store details of previous incidents, problems, workarounds, root causes and their resolutions
- Functionality to categorize and quickly retrieve previous known errors, using pattern matching and keyword searching against symptoms
- Multi-level diagnostic scripts to allow service desk staff to pinpoint the cause of failures. These context-sensitive scripts appear on screens, dependent upon the multi-level categorization of the incident, and are driven by the user's answers to diagnostic questions

■ Automated 'self-help' functionality so users can seek and
obtain help to resolve their own difficulties. Ideally this should
be a 24/7 web interface driven by menu selection: for example,
frequently asked questions; 'how to do' search capabilities;
password change or software repairs and fixes. Self-help may
also include allowing users to log incidents themselves
■ Remote control of the user's desktop to allow service desk
analysts to conduct investigations or correct settings
■ Appropriate IT service continuity and resilience levels.

9.4 PRACTICES FOR PROCESS IMPLEMENTATION

9.4.1 Service operation and project management (SO 8.2)

It is important that all projects make use of project management
processes. Many organizations treat service operation as
'business as usual' and do not use project management for
activities such as major infrastructure upgrades or deployment of
new or changed procedures.

Using project management processes can bring the
following benefits:

■ Project benefits are agreed and documented
■ It is easier to see what is being done and how it is
being managed
■ Funding can be easier to obtain
■ There is greater consistency and improved quality
■ Objectives are more likely to be achieved, leading to higher
credibility for operational groups.

9.4.2 Assessing and managing risk in service operation (SO 8.3)

Risk assessment and management is required throughout the service lifecycle. There are occasions, such as the following, when assessment of risk to service operation must be carried out and acted on very quickly:

- Risks from potential changes or known errors
- Failures or potential failures: these may be identified by event management, incident management or problem management, but also by warnings from manufacturers, suppliers or contractors
- Environmental risks: risks to the physical environment as well as political, commercial or industrial relations risks, which could lead to invoking IT service continuity
- Suppliers, particularly if they control key service components
- Security risks
- Support of new customers or services.

9.4.3 Operational staff in service design and transition (SO 8.4)

Activities during service design and service transition should involve staff from all IT groups to ensure that new components and services are designed, tested and implemented in a way that will provide the service utility and service warranty required.

Service operation staff must be involved during the early stages of design and transition to ensure that new services are fit for purpose from an operational perspective and supportable in the future. This will mean that:

- Services are capable of being supported from a technical and operational viewpoint with existing (or agreed additional) resources and skills
- There is no adverse impact on other practices, processes or schedules
- There are no unexpected operational costs
- There are no unexpected contractual or legal complications
- There are no complex support paths with multiple support departments or third parties.

Planning changes, and implementing them, does not involve technology alone. Thought must be given to awareness, cultural change, motivation and many other issues.

9.5   CHALLENGES, CRITICAL SUCCESS FACTORS AND RISKS RELATING TO IMPLEMENTING PRACTICES AND PROCESSES

9.5.1   Challenges (ST 9.1, SO 9.1, SD 9.1)

There are a number of challenges faced within service operation that need to be overcome. These include:

- Lack of engagement with development and project staff. While it is good to have segregation of duties, involving service operations staff at the outset of development projects is good for both teams
- Justifying funding: while it is often difficult to justify expenditure in the area of service operation, in reality, such an investment can show a positive return on investment and improvement in service quality; for example, reduced software licence costs and reduced support costs due to fewer incidents

- Challenges for service operation managers, such as differing perspectives of projects and operations, ineffective transitions and managing virtual teams
- Unreasonable targets and timescales, as previously agreed in the SLAs and OLAs
- Normal daily operation or business as usual not having been considered as part of the design
- Poor supplier management and/or poor supplier performance
- Achieving a balance between maintaining a stable production environment and being responsive to the business needs for changing the services
- Insufficient knowledge transfer and training during service transition.

9.5.2   Critical success factors (SD 9.3, ST 9.2, SO 9.2)

CSFs to consider include:

- **Management support** Senior and middle management support is needed for all ITSM activities and processes, particularly in service operation; for example, for funding and resourcing, for new initiatives and for empowerment of middle managers
- **Business support** Regular communications with the business to understand its concerns and aspirations and to give feedback on efforts to meet its needs are essential in building the correct relationships and ensuring ongoing support
- **Champions** ITSM projects and the resulting service operation are more successful if there are 'champions' who lead and encourage others with their enthusiasm and commitment. These champions are usually senior managers, but successful champions can also come from other parts of the organization

- ■ **Staffing and retention** Having the appropriate number of staff with the appropriate skills is critical to the success of service operation. Challenges include lack of staff with an understanding of service management, difficulty of retaining staff and workload management
- ■ **Service management training** In addition to generic service management training, staff should be trained on:
  - – The organization's own processes that have been implemented
  - – People skills, especially for those in customer-facing positions
  - – Understanding the business and the required service culture
  - – Service management tools
- ■ **Suitable tools** Many service operation processes and activities cannot be performed effectively without adequate support tools. Senior management must provide funding for procurement, deployment and ongoing maintenance of these
- ■ **Validity of testing** The quality of IT services provided is dependent upon the quality of systems and components delivered to the operational environment, requiring adequate and complete testing of new components and releases and documentation testing for completeness and quality
- ■ **Measurement and reporting** Clear definitions of how things will be measured and reported will provide staff with targets to aim for and allow IT and business managers to review progress and identify opportunities for improvement.

Other CSFs include defining clear accountabilities, roles and responsibilities, establishing a culture that enables knowledge to be shared freely and willingly, demonstrating continual improvements and improved customer and user satisfaction ratings.

9.5.3   Risks (ST 9.3, SO 9.3, SD 9.2)

In addition to not meeting the challenges and not addressing the CSFs above, other risks are:

■ Service loss: the ultimate risk to the business of weaknesses in service operation is the loss of critical IT services with subsequent adverse impact on employees, customers and finances
■ Resistance to change and circumvention of the processes due to perceived bureaucracy
■ Lack of maturity and integration of systems and tools, resulting in people 'blaming' technology for other shortcomings
■ Poor integration between the processes, causing process isolation and a silo approach to delivering ITSM.

Additional risks to successful service operation include inadequate funding and resources, loss of key personnel, faulty initial design and differing customer expectations.

9.6   PLANNING AND IMPLEMENTING SERVICE MANAGEMENT TECHNOLOGIES (SO 8.5)

There are a number of factors to consider when deploying and implementing ITSM support tools:

■ **Licences** The cost of service management tools is usually determined by the type and number of user licences needed. Most tools are modular, so the specific selection of modules also affects the price. It is important to plan the provision of licences to avoid unexpected costs. There are a number of different licence types:
  – **Dedicated licences** For staff who need frequent and prolonged use of the module (e.g. service desk staff)

- **Shared licences** For staff who use the module regularly, but with significant times when it is not needed. The ratio of licences to users should be calculated to give sufficient use at acceptable cost
- **Web licences** For staff who need occasional access, or remote access, or who only need limited functionality
- **Service on demand** The charge is based on the number of hours the service is used. This is suitable for smaller organizations or very specialized tools that are not used often. It can also include tools licensed as part of a consulting exercise (e.g. for carrying out capacity modelling)

■ **Deployment** Many tools, especially discovery and event-monitoring tools, require deployment of clients or agents. This requires careful scheduling, planning and execution and should be subject to formal release and deployment management. Devices may need to be rebooted and this needs to be planned. Change management is used and the CMS updated. Particular care should be taken when planning deployment to laptops and other portable equipment that may not be connected all the time

■ **Capacity checks** It may be necessary to check for sufficient system resources (e.g. disk space, CPU, memory) when planning a deployment. Allow sufficient lead time for upgrading or replacing equipment, and check network capacity

■ **Timing of technology deployment** If tools are deployed too early, they can be seen as 'the solution' on their own and essential process improvements will not be carried out. If tools are deployed too late, it can be hard to implement the new process. People need to be trained in use of the tool as well as the new or updated process, and timing for this must be planned, possibly with additional training after the tools have gone live

- **Type of introduction** The new tool often replaces an existing tool, and careful planning is needed for the transition. A phased approach can be more appropriate than a 'big bang' approach, but this depends on the exact circumstances. The key factor is planning what data needs to be migrated, and how. If data is being migrated, a data quality audit should be performed. An alternative approach is parallel running, in which case the old tool should run in a 'read only' mode to prevent mistakes.

10 Qualifications

10.1 OVERVIEW

The ITIL qualification scheme has four levels:

- Foundation level
- Intermediate level (Lifecycle and Capability streams)
- ITIL Expert
- ITIL Master.

There are also further complementary service management qualifications available that can contribute (accumulating credits) towards achievement of the ITIL Expert. Further details of these can be found at:

www.itil-officialsite.com/Qualifications/
ComplementaryQualifications.aspx

10.2 FOUNDATION LEVEL

The Foundation level ensures candidates gain knowledge of the ITIL terminology, structure and basic concepts, and comprehend the core principles of ITIL practices for service management. Foundation represents two credits towards the ITIL Expert.

10.3 INTERMEDIATE LEVEL

There are two streams in the Intermediate level, assessing an individual's ability to analyse and apply concepts of ITIL:

- Lifecycle stream
- Capability stream.

10.3.1 Lifecycle stream

The Lifecycle stream is built around the five core publications and is for candidates wanting to gain knowledge within the service lifecycle context. Each module achieves three credits.

10.3.2 Capability stream

The Capability stream is built around four practitioner-based clusters and is for candidates wanting to gain knowledge of specific processes and roles. Each module achieves four credits:

- **Planning, protection and optimization (PPO)** Including capacity management, availability management, IT service continuity management, information security management, and demand management
- **Service offerings and agreements (SOA)** Including service portfolio management, service level management, service catalogue management, demand management, supplier management, and financial management for IT services
- **Release, control and validation (RCV)** Including change management, release and deployment management, service validation and testing, service asset and configuration management, knowledge management, request fulfilment, and change evaluation
- **Operational support and analysis (OSA)** Including event management, incident management, request fulfilment, problem management, access management, service desk, technical management, IT operations management and application management.

Candidates may take units from either of the streams to accumulate credits.

To complete the Intermediate level, the Managing Across the Lifecycle course (five credits) is required to bring together the full essence of a lifecycle approach to service management, consolidating knowledge gained across the qualification scheme.

10.4 ITIL EXPERT

Candidates automatically qualify for an ITIL Expert certificate once they have achieved the prerequisite 22 credits from Foundation (the mandatory initial unit) and Intermediate units (including Managing Across the Lifecycle, the mandatory final unit). No further examinations or courses are required.

10.5 ITIL MASTER

The ITIL Master qualification validates the capability of the candidate to apply the principles, methods and techniques of ITIL in the workplace.

To achieve the ITIL Master qualification, the candidate must be able to explain and justify how they selected and individually applied a range of knowledge, principles, methods and techniques from ITIL and supporting management techniques, to achieve desired business outcomes in one or more practical assignments.

To be eligible for the ITIL Master qualification, candidates must have reached the ITIL Expert level and worked in IT service management for at least five years in leadership, managerial or higher-management advisory levels.

11 Related guidance (SO Appendix A)

This chapter summarizes the frameworks, best practices, standards, models and quality systems that complement ITIL practices.

11.1 ITIL GUIDANCE AND WEB SERVICES

ITIL is part of the Best Management Practice portfolio, published by TSO. Further information can be found at:

www.best-management-practice.com

and on the official ITIL site at: www.itil-officialsite.com

The ITIL glossary is accessed via the official ITIL site.

11.2 QUALITY MANAGEMENT SYSTEM

It is helpful to align service management processes with any quality management system already present in an organization. Total Quality Management (TQM) and ISO 9000:2005 are widely used, as is the Plan-Do-Check-Act (PDCA) cycle, often referred to as the Deming Cycle.

More information can be found at www.iso.org and www.deming.org

11.3 RISK MANAGEMENT

Every organization should implement some form of risk management, appropriate to its size and needs. Risk is usually defined as 'uncertainty of outcome', and can have both positive and negative effects. *Management of Risk* (M_o_R®), ISO 31000,

Risk IT and ISO/IEC 27001 all provide guidance related to risk management. See Appendix G in *ITIL Service Operation* (Cabinet Office, 2011) for further description of risk management.

11.4 GOVERNANCE OF IT

Governance defines the rules, policies and processes an organization needs to follow, and makes sure they are implemented consistently.

There are two ISO standards that relate to governance. ISO 9004 provides board and executive level guidance, and ISO/IEC 38500 provides for corporate governance.

11.5 COBIT

Control OBjectives for Information and related Technology (COBIT) is a governance and control framework for IT management. COBIT looks at what needs to be achieved, and ITIL provides complementary guidance about how to achieve it.

Further information can be found at www.isaca.org and www.itgi.org

11.6 ISO/IEC 20000 SERVICE MANAGEMENT SERIES

ISO/IEC 20000 is the standard for ITSM, applying to both internal and external service providers, although the standard is currently to be extended with the development of Parts 3 and 4:

- ISO/IEC 20000-1:2011 Part 1: Service management system requirements
- ISO/IEC 20000-2:2012 Part 2: Guidance on the application of service management systems

- ISO/IEC 20000-3:2012 Part 3: Guidance on scope definition and applicability of ISO/IEC 20000-1
- ISO/IEC 20000-4:2007 Part 4: Process reference model
- ISO/IEC 20000-5:2010 Part 5: Exemplar implementation plan for ISO/IEC 20000-1
- BIP 0005: A manager's guide to service management
- BIP 0015: IT service management: self-assessment workbook (currently assesses against ITIL V2, to be revised via ITIL V3 complementary publications).

These documents provide a standard against which organizations can be assessed and certified with regard to the quality of their ITSM processes.

An ISO/IEC 20000 certification scheme was introduced in December 2005. A number of auditing organizations are accredited within the scheme to assess and certify organizations as compliant to the ISO/IEC 20000 standard and its content. The standard and ITIL are aligned, and ITIL best practices can help an organization looking to achieve ISO accreditation.

Further information can be found at www.iso.org or www.isoiec20000certification.com

11.7   ENVIRONMENTAL MANAGEMENT AND GREEN AND SUSTAINABLE IT

IT is a major user of energy, but can also support cultural and environmental changes as part of a green initiative. Green IT is about environmentally sustainable computing, from design through to disposal.

ISO 14001 is a series of standards related to an environment management system. Further details can be found at www.iso.org

11.8 ISO STANDARDS AND PUBLICATIONS FOR IT

There are many ISO standards and publications with relevance for IT and ITIL. Further details can be found at www.iso.org

Relevant examples include:

- ISO 9241: covers aspects that may affect the utility of a service
- ISO/IEC JTC1: deals with IT standards and publications
- The SC27 sub-committee develops ISO/IEC 27000, which relates to information security management
- The SC7 sub-committee develops other relevant standards including ISO/IEC 20000 (service management), ISO/IEC 15504 (process assessment or SPICE) and ISO/IEC 19770 (software asset management).

11.9 ITIL AND THE OSI FRAMEWORK

The Open Systems Interconnection (OSI) framework was developed by ISO at the same time as ITIL V1 was written. Common expressions such as installation, moves, additions and changes (IMAC) are OSI terminology, although IT practitioners may not realize this.

11.10 PROGRAMME AND PROJECT MANAGEMENT

Programme management can be used to deliver complex pieces of work, using interrelated projects. *Managing Successful Programmes* (MSP®) provides guidance related to programme management.

Portfolio, Programme and Project Offices (P3O®) provides guidance on managing these three areas together.

Project management guidance is found in PRojects IN Controlled Environments (PRINCE2®) and the Project Management Body of Knowledge (PMBOK).

Details of the above publications can be found at:

www.msp-officialsite.com

www.p3o-officialsite.com

www.prince-officialsite.com

www.pmi.org

11.11 ORGANIZATIONAL CHANGE

The organizational aspects of IT change need to be considered to ensure that changes are successful. Kotter's eight steps for organizational change (www.johnkotter.com) are referenced in *ITIL Service Transition* and *ITIL Continual Service Improvement* (Cabinet Office, 2011). See section on further guidance for details.

11.12 SKILLS FRAMEWORK FOR THE INFORMATION AGE

Skills Framework for the Information Age (SFIA) provides a common framework for IT skills. This supports job standardization, skills audits and skills planning exercises.

SFIA is a two-dimensional matrix showing areas of work and levels of responsibility. Further information can be found at www.sfia-online.org

11.13 CARNEGIE MELLON: CMMI AND eSCM FRAMEWORKS

The Capability Maturity Model Integration (CMMI) is a process improvement approach applicable to projects, divisions or entire organizations.

The eSourcing Capability Model for Service Providers (eSCM-SP) is a framework to improve the relationship between IT service providers and customers.

SCAMPI assessments can be carried out against CMMI–Standard CMMI Appraisal Method for Process Improvement. More information can be found at www.cmmiinstitute.com

11.14 BALANCED SCORECARD

The balanced scorecard approach to strategic management was developed by Drs Robert Kaplan and David Norton. It views an organization from four perspectives to balance out the financial perspective which drives many decisions. The perspectives are:

- Learning and growth
- Business process
- Customer
- Financial.

The scorecard can be applied to IT quality performance and service operation performance. More information can be found at www.scorecardsupport.com

11.15 SIX SIGMA

Six Sigma is a data-driven process improvement approach. It identifies defects that lead to improvement opportunities. Six Sigma tries to reduce process variation. It has two primary sub-methodologies:

■ DMAIC – define, measure, analyse, improve, control
■ DMADV – define, measure, analyse, design, verify.

Further information can be found online, including Six Sigma overviews and training.

Further guidance and contact points

TSO

PO Box 29
Norwich NR3 1GN
United Kingdom
Tel: +44(0) 870 600 5522
Fax: +44(0) 870 600 5533
Email: customer.services@tso.co.uk
www.tso.co.uk

_it_SMF UK

150 Wharfedale Road
Winnersh Triangle
Wokingham
Berkshire RG41 5RB
United Kingdom
Tel: +44(0) 118 918 6500
Fax: +44(0) 118 969 9749
Email: publications@itsmf.co.uk
www.itsmf.co.uk

BEST PRACTICE WITH ITIL

The ITIL publication portfolio consists of a unique library of titles that offer guidance on quality IT services and best practices. The ITIL 2011 lifecycle suite (five core publications) comprises:

Cabinet Office (2011). *ITIL Service Strategy*. The Stationery Office, London.

Cabinet Office (2011). *ITIL Service Design*. The Stationery Office, London.

Cabinet Office (2011). *ITIL Service Transition*. The Stationery Office, London.

Cabinet Office (2011). *ITIL Service Operation*. The Stationery Office, London.

Cabinet Office (2011). *ITIL Continual Service Improvement*. The Stationery Office, London.

ITIL-DERIVED GUIDANCE

There is a range of derived publications which support the core guidance. Details of all publications can be found in the publications library section of the Best Management Practice website: www.best-management-practice.com/Publications-Library/IT-Service-Management-ITIL

ABOUT *it*SMF

*it*SMF is the only truly independent and internationally recognized forum for IT service management professionals worldwide. Since 1991 this not-for-profit organization has been a prominent player in the ongoing development and promotion of IT service management best practice, standards and qualifications. Globally, *it*SMF now boasts more than 6,000 member companies, blue-chip and public-sector alike, covering in excess of 70,000 individuals spread over more than 50 international chapters.

Each chapter is a separate legal entity and is largely autonomous. *it*SMF International provides an overall steering and support function to existing and emerging chapters. It has its own website at www.itsmfi.org

The UK chapter has more than 8,000 members: it offers a flourishing annual conference, online bookstore, regular regional meetings, seminars and special interest groups and numerous other benefits for members. Its website is at www.itsmf.co.uk

ABOUT TSO

TSO is one of the largest publishers by volume in the UK, publishing more than 9,000 titles a year in print and digital formats for a wide range of clients.

TSO has a long history in publishing best-practice guidance related to project, programme and IT service management. Working with partners including *it*SMF, the Project Management Institute, Service Management 101 and APMG-International, we publish guidance for a global range of management disciplines.

For more information on our publications and to browse our resources, please visit www.internationalbestpractice.com

Glossary

A candidate is expected to understand the following terms after completing an OSA course.

These terms are as defined in the standard ITIL glossary. The core publication titles (*ITIL Service Strategy, ITIL Service Design, ITIL Service Operation, ITIL Service Transition* and *ITIL Continual Service Improvement)* included in parentheses at the beginning of the definition indicate where a reader can find more information.

active monitoring

(*ITIL Service Operation*) Monitoring of a configuration item or an IT service that uses automated regular checks to discover the current status. *See also* passive monitoring.

alert

(*ITIL Service Operation*) A notification that a threshold has been reached, something has changed, or a failure has occurred. Alerts are often created and managed by system management tools and are managed by the event management process.

application

Software that provides functions which are required by an IT service. Each application may be part of more than one IT service. An application runs on one or more servers or clients.

automatic call distribution (ACD)

(*ITIL Service Operation*) Use of information technology to direct an incoming telephone call to the most appropriate person in the shortest possible time. ACD is sometimes called automated call distribution.

availability

(*ITIL Service Design*) Ability of an IT service or other configuration item to perform its agreed function when required. Availability is determined by reliability, maintainability, serviceability, performance and security. Availability is usually calculated as a percentage. This calculation is often based on agreed service time and downtime. It is best practice to calculate availability of an IT service using measurements of the business output.

back-out

(*ITIL Service Transition*) An activity that restores a service or other configuration item to a previous baseline. Back-out is used as a form of remediation when a change or release is not successful.

budgeting

The activity of predicting and controlling the spending of money. Budgeting consists of a periodic negotiation cycle to set future budgets (usually annual) and the day-to-day monitoring and adjusting of current budgets.

business case

(*ITIL Service Strategy*) Justification for a significant item of expenditure. The business case includes information about costs, benefits, options, issues, risks and possible problems.

business objective

(*ITIL Service Strategy*) The objective of a business process, or of the business as a whole. Business objectives support the business vision, provide guidance for the IT strategy, and are often supported by IT services.

business relationship management

(*ITIL Service Strategy*) The process responsible for maintaining a positive relationship with customers. Business relationship management identifies customer needs and ensures that the service provider is able to meet these needs with an appropriate catalogue of services. This process has strong links with service level management.

call

(*ITIL Service Operation*) A telephone call to the service desk from a user. A call could result in an incident or a service request being logged.

call centre

(*ITIL Service Operation*) An organization or business unit that handles large numbers of incoming and outgoing telephone calls.

call type

(*ITIL Service Operation*) A category that is used to distinguish incoming requests to a service desk. Common call types are incident, service request and complaint.

capacity

(*ITIL Service Design*) The maximum throughput that a configuration item or IT service can deliver. For some types of CI, capacity may be the size or volume – for example, a disk drive.

change advisory board (CAB)

(*ITIL Service Transition*) A group of people that support the assessment, prioritization, authorization and scheduling of changes. A change advisory board is usually made up of representatives from: all areas within the IT service provider; the business; and third parties such as suppliers.

change schedule

(*ITIL Service Transition*) A document that lists all authorized changes and their planned implementation dates, as well as the estimated dates of longer-term changes. A change schedule is sometimes called a forward schedule of change, even though it also contains information about changes that have already been implemented.

computer telephony integration (CTI)

(*ITIL Service Operation*) Computer telephony integration is a general term covering any kind of integration between computers and telephone systems. It is most commonly used to refer to systems where an application displays detailed screens relating to incoming or outgoing telephone calls. *See also* automatic call distribution; interactive voice response.

configuration item (CI)

(*ITIL Service Transition*) Any component or other service asset that needs to be managed in order to deliver an IT service. Information about each configuration item is recorded in a configuration record within the configuration management system and is maintained throughout its lifecycle by service asset and configuration management. Configuration items are under the control of change management. They typically include IT services, hardware, software, buildings, people and formal documentation such as process documentation and service level agreements.

configuration management system (CMS)

(*ITIL Service Transition*) A set of tools, data and information that is used to support service asset and configuration management. The CMS is part of an overall service knowledge management system and includes tools for collecting, storing, managing, updating, analysing and presenting data about all configuration items and their relationships. The CMS may also include information about incidents, problems, known errors, changes and releases. The CMS is maintained by service asset and configuration management and is used by all IT service management processes.

continual service improvement (CSI)

(*ITIL Continual Service Improvement*) A stage in the lifecycle of a service. Continual service improvement ensures that services are aligned with changing business needs by identifying and implementing improvements to IT services that support business processes. The performance of the IT service provider is continually measured and improvements are made to processes, IT services and IT infrastructure in order to increase efficiency, effectiveness and cost effectiveness. Continual service improvement includes the seven-step improvement process. Although this process is associated with continual service improvement, most processes have activities that take place across multiple stages of the service lifecycle.

customer-facing service

(*ITIL Service Design*) An IT service that is visible to the customer. These are normally services that support the customer's business processes and facilitate one or more outcomes desired by the customer. All live customer-facing services, including those available for deployment, are recorded in the service catalogue along with customer-visible information about deliverables, prices, contact points, ordering and request processes. Other information such as relationships to supporting services and other CIs will also be recorded for internal use by the IT service provider.

dashboard

(*ITIL Service Operation*) A graphical representation of overall IT service performance and availability. Dashboard images may be updated in real time, and can also be included in management reports and web pages. Dashboards can be used to support service level management, event management and incident diagnosis.

detection

(*ITIL Service Operation*) A stage in the expanded incident lifecycle. Detection results in the incident becoming known to the service provider. Detection can be automatic or the result of a user logging an incident.

diagnosis

(*ITIL Service Operation*) A stage in the incident and problem lifecycles. The purpose of diagnosis is to identify a workaround for an incident or the root cause of a problem.

diagnostic script

(*ITIL Service Operation*) A structured set of questions used by service desk staff to ensure they ask the correct questions, and to help them classify, resolve and assign incidents. Diagnostic scripts may also be made available to users to help them diagnose and resolve their own incidents.

downtime

(*ITIL Service Design*) (*ITIL Service Operation*) The time when an IT service or other configuration item is not available during its agreed service time. The availability of an IT service is often calculated from agreed service time and downtime.

early life support

(*ITIL Service Transition*) A stage in the service lifecycle that occurs at the end of deployment and before the service is fully accepted into operation. During early life support, the service provider reviews key performance indicators, service levels and monitoring thresholds and may implement improvements to ensure that service targets can be met. The service provider may also provide additional resources for incident and problem management during this time.

error

(*ITIL Service Operation*) A design flaw or malfunction that causes a failure of one or more IT services or other configuration items. A mistake made by a person or a faulty process that impacts a configuration item is also an error.

escalation

(*ITIL Service Operation*) An activity that obtains additional resources when these are needed to meet service level targets or customer expectations. Escalation may be needed within any IT service management process, but is most commonly associated with incident management, problem management and the management of customer complaints. There are two types of escalation: functional escalation and hierarchic escalation.

event

(*ITIL Service Operation*) A change of state that has significance for the management of an IT service or other configuration item. The term is also used to mean an alert or notification created by any IT service, configuration item or monitoring tool. Events typically require IT operations personnel to take actions, and often lead to incidents being logged.

failure

(*ITIL Service Operation*) Loss of ability to operate to specification, or to deliver the required output. The term may be used when referring to IT services, processes, activities, configuration items etc. A failure often causes an incident.

first-line support

(*ITIL Service Operation*) The first level in a hierarchy of support groups involved in the resolution of incidents. Each level contains more specialist skills, or has more time or other resources. *See also* escalation.

follow the sun

(*ITIL Service Operation*) A methodology for using service desks and support groups around the world to provide seamless 24/7 service. Calls, incidents, problems and service requests are passed between groups in different time zones.

fulfilment

Performing activities to meet a need or requirement – for example, by providing a new IT service, or meeting a service request.

function

A team or group of people and the tools or other resources that they use to carry out one or more processes or activities – for example, the service desk. The term also has two other meanings:

■ An intended purpose of a configuration item, person, team, process or IT service. For example, one function of an email service may be to store and forward outgoing messages, while the function of a business process may be to despatch goods to customers.
■ To perform the intended purpose correctly, as in 'The computer is functioning'.

functional escalation

(*ITIL Service Operation*) Transferring an incident, problem or change to a technical team with a higher level of expertise to assist in an escalation.

hierarchic escalation

(*ITIL Service Operation*) Informing or involving more senior levels of management to assist in an escalation.

identity

(*ITIL Service Operation*) A unique name that is used to identify a user, person or role. The identity is used to grant rights to that user, person or role. Examples of identities might be the username SmithJ or the role 'change manager'.

impact

(*ITIL Service Operation*) (*ITIL Service Transition*) A measure of the effect of an incident, problem or change on business processes. Impact is often based on how service levels will be affected. Impact and urgency are used to assign priority.

incident

(*ITIL Service Operation*) An unplanned interruption to an IT service or reduction in the quality of an IT service. Failure of a configuration item that has not yet affected service is also an incident – for example, failure of one disk from a mirror set.

incident record

(*ITIL Service Operation*) A record containing the details of an incident. Each incident record documents the lifecycle of a single incident.

information security management

(*ITIL Service Design*) The process responsible for ensuring that the confidentiality, integrity and availability of an organization's assets, information, data and IT services match the agreed needs of the business. Information security management supports business security and has a wider scope than that of the IT service provider, and includes handling of paper, building access, phone calls etc. for the entire organization.

information security policy

(*ITIL Service Design*) The policy that governs the organization's approach to information security management.

interactive voice response (IVR)

(*ITIL Service Operation*) A form of automatic call distribution that accepts user input, such as key presses and spoken commands, to identify the correct destination for incoming calls.

Ishikawa diagram

(*ITIL Continual Service Improvement*) (*ITIL Service Operation*) A technique that helps a team to identify all the possible causes of a problem. Originally devised by Kaoru Ishikawa, the output of this technique is a diagram that looks like a fishbone.

IT operations

(*ITIL Service Operation*) Activities carried out by IT operations control, including console management/operations bridge, job scheduling, backup and restore, and print and output management. IT operations is also used as a synonym for service operation.

IT operations control

(*ITIL Service Operation*) The function responsible for monitoring and control of the IT services and IT infrastructure. *See also* operations bridge.

IT operations management

(*ITIL Service Operation*) The function within an IT service provider that performs the daily activities needed to manage IT services and the supporting IT infrastructure. IT operations management includes IT operations control and facilities management.

IT service continuity plan

(*ITIL Service Design*) A plan defining the steps required to recover one or more IT services. The plan also identifies the triggers for invocation, people to be involved, communications etc. The IT service continuity plan should be part of a business continuity plan.

job scheduling

(*ITIL Service Operation*) Planning and managing the execution of software tasks that are required as part of an IT service. Job scheduling is carried out by IT operations management, and is often automated using software tools that run batch or online tasks at specific times of the day, week, month or year.

Kepner and Tregoe analysis

(*ITIL Service Operation*) A structured approach to problem solving. The problem is analysed in terms of what, where, when and extent. Possible causes are identified, the most probable cause is tested, and the true cause is verified.

key performance indicator (KPI)

(*ITIL Continual Service Improvement*) (*ITIL Service Design*) A metric that is used to help manage an IT service, process, plan, project or other activity. Key performance indicators are used to measure the achievement of critical success factors. Many metrics may be measured, but only the most important of these are defined as key performance indicators and used to actively manage and report on the process, IT service or activity. They should be selected to ensure that efficiency, effectiveness and cost effectiveness are all managed.

known error

(*ITIL Service Operation*) A problem that has a documented root cause and a workaround. Known errors are created and managed throughout their lifecycle by problem management. Known errors may also be identified by development or suppliers.

known error database (KEDB)

(*ITIL Service Operation*) A database containing all known error records. This database is created by problem management and used by incident and problem management. The known error database may be part of the configuration management system, or may be stored elsewhere in the service knowledge management system.

live environment

(*ITIL Service Transition*) A controlled environment containing live configuration items used to deliver IT services to customers.

major incident

(*ITIL Service Operation*) The highest category of impact for an incident. A major incident results in significant disruption to the business.

manageability

An informal measure of how easily and effectively an IT service or other component can be managed.

middleware

(*ITIL Service Design*) Software that connects two or more software components or applications. Middleware is usually purchased from a supplier, rather than developed within the IT service provider.

monitoring

(*ITIL Service Operation*) Repeated observation of a configuration item, IT service or process to detect events and to ensure that the current status is known.

normal service operation

(*ITIL Service Operation*) An operational state where services and configuration items are performing within their agreed service and operational levels.

operation

(*ITIL Service Operation*) Day-to-day management of an IT service, system or other configuration item. Operation is also used to mean any predefined activity or transaction – for example, loading a magnetic tape, accepting money at a point of sale, or reading data from a disk drive.

operational level agreement

(*ITIL Continual Service Improvement*) (*ITIL Service Design*) An agreement between an IT service provider and another part of the same organization. It supports the IT service provider's delivery of IT services to customers and defines the goods or services to be provided and the responsibilities of both parties. For example, there could be an operational level agreement:

- Between the IT service provider and a procurement department to obtain hardware in agreed times
- Between the service desk and a support group to provide incident resolution in agreed times.

See also service level agreement.

operations bridge

(*ITIL Service Operation*) A physical location where IT services and IT infrastructure are monitored and managed.

outcome

The result of carrying out an activity, following a process, or delivering an IT service etc. The term is used to refer to intended results as well as to actual results.

pain value analysis

(*ITIL Service Operation*) A technique used to help identify the business impact of one or more problems. A formula is used to calculate pain value based on the number of users affected, the duration of the downtime, the impact on each user, and the cost to the business (if known).

Pareto principle

(*ITIL Service Operation*) A technique used to prioritize activities. The Pareto principle says that 80% of the value of any activity is created with 20% of the effort. Pareto analysis is also used in problem management to prioritize possible problem causes for investigation.

passive monitoring

(*ITIL Service Operation*) Monitoring of a configuration item, an IT service or a process that relies on an alert or notification to discover the current status. *See also* active monitoring.

priority

(*ITIL Service Operation*) (*ITIL Service Transition*) A category used to identify the relative importance of an incident, problem or change. Priority is based on impact and urgency, and is used to identify required times for actions to be taken. For example, the service level agreement may state that Priority 2 incidents must be resolved within 12 hours.

proactive problem management

(*ITIL Service Operation*) Part of the problem management process. The objective of proactive problem management is to identify problems that might otherwise be missed. Proactive problem management analyses incident records, and uses data collected by other IT service management processes to identify trends or significant problems.

problem

(*ITIL Service Operation*) A cause of one or more incidents. The cause is not usually known at the time a problem record is created, and the problem management process is responsible for further investigation.

problem record

(*ITIL Service Operation*) A record containing the details of a problem. Each problem record documents the lifecycle of a single problem.

project

A temporary organization, with people and other assets, that is required to achieve an objective or other outcome. Each project has a lifecycle that typically includes initiation, planning, execution, and closure. Projects are usually managed using a formal methodology such as PRojects IN Controlled Environments (PRINCE2) or the Project Management Body of Knowledge (PMBOK).

projected service outage (PSO)

(*ITIL Service Transition*) A document that identifies the effect of planned changes, maintenance activities and test plans on agreed service levels.

recovery

(*ITIL Service Design*) (*ITIL Service Operation*) Returning a configuration item or an IT service to a working state. Recovery of an IT service often includes recovering data to a known consistent state. After recovery, further steps may be needed before the IT service can be made available to the users (restoration).

request model

(*ITIL Service Operation*) A repeatable way of dealing with a particular category of service request. A request model defines specific agreed steps that will be followed for a service request of this category. Request models may be very simple, with no requirement for authorization (e.g. password reset), or may be more complex with many steps that require authorization (e.g. provision of an existing IT service).

resolution

(*ITIL Service Operation*) Action taken to repair the root cause of an incident or problem, or to implement a workaround. In ISO/IEC 20000, resolution processes is the process group that includes incident and problem management.

response time

A measure of the time taken to complete an operation or transaction. Used in capacity management as a measure of IT infrastructure performance, and in incident management as a measure of the time taken to answer the phone, or to start diagnosis.

restore

(*ITIL Service Operation*) Taking action to return an IT service to the users after repair and recovery from an incident. This is the primary objective of incident management.

risk management

The process responsible for identifying, assessing and controlling risks. Risk management is also sometimes used to refer to the second part of the overall process after risks have been identified and assessed, as in 'risk assessment and management'. This process is not described in detail within the core ITIL publications.

root cause

(*ITIL Service Operation*) The underlying or original cause of an incident or problem.

root cause analysis (RCA)

(*ITIL Service Operation*) An activity that identifies the root cause of an incident or problem. Root cause analysis typically concentrates on IT infrastructure failures.

second-line support

(*ITIL Service Operation*) The second level in a hierarchy of support groups involved in the resolution of incidents and investigation of problems. Each level contains more specialist skills, or is allocated more time or other resources.

service asset and configuration management

(*ITIL Service Transition*) The process responsible for ensuring that the assets required to deliver services are properly controlled, and that accurate and reliable information about those assets is available when and where it is needed. This information includes details of how the assets have been configured and the relationships between assets. *See also* configuration management system.

service catalogue

(*ITIL Service Design*) (*ITIL Service Strategy*) A database or structured document with information about all live IT services, including those available for deployment. The service catalogue is part of the service portfolio and contains information about two types of IT service: customer-facing services that are visible to the business; and supporting services required by the service provider to deliver customer-facing services.

service design

(*ITIL Service Design*) A stage in the lifecycle of a service. Service design includes the design of the services, governing practices, processes and policies required to realize the service provider's strategy and to facilitate the introduction of services into supported environments. Service design includes the following processes: design coordination, service catalogue management, service level management, availability management, capacity management, IT service continuity management, information security management, and supplier management. Although these processes are associated with service design, most processes have activities that take place across multiple stages of the service lifecycle.

service hours

(*ITIL Service Design*) An agreed time period when a particular IT service should be available. For example, 'Monday–Friday 08:00 to 17:00 except public holidays'. Service hours should be defined in a service level agreement.

service knowledge management system (SKMS)

(*ITIL Service Transition*) A set of tools and databases that is used to manage knowledge, information and data. The service knowledge management system includes the configuration management system, as well as other databases and information systems. The service knowledge management system includes tools for collecting, storing, managing, updating, analysing and presenting all the knowledge, information and data that an IT service provider will need to manage the full lifecycle of IT services.

service level agreement (SLA)

(*ITIL Continual Service Improvement*) (*ITIL Service Design*) An agreement between an IT service provider and a customer. A service level agreement describes the IT service, documents service level targets, and specifies the responsibilities of the IT service provider and the customer. A single agreement may cover multiple IT services or multiple customers. *See also* operational level agreement.

service level target

(*ITIL Continual Service Improvement*) (*ITIL Service Design*) A commitment that is documented in a service level agreement. Service level targets are based on service level requirements, and are needed to ensure that the IT service design is fit for purpose. They should be SMART, and are usually based on key performance indicators.

service portfolio

(*ITIL Service Strategy*) The complete set of services that are managed by a service provider. The service portfolio is used to manage the entire lifecycle of all services, and includes three categories: service pipeline (proposed or in development), service catalogue (live or available for deployment) and retired services.

service request

(*ITIL Service Operation*) A formal request from a user for something to be provided – for example, a request for information or advice; to reset a password; or to install a workstation for a new user. Service requests are managed by the request fulfilment process, usually in conjunction with the service desk. Service requests may be linked to a request for change as part of fulfilling the request.

shift

(*ITIL Service Operation*) A group or team of people who carry out a specific role for a fixed period of time. For example, there could be four shifts of IT operations control personnel to support an IT service that is used 24 hours a day.

single point of contact

(*ITIL Service Operation*) Providing a single consistent way to communicate with an organization or business unit. For example, a single point of contact for an IT service provider is usually called a service desk.

standard change

(*ITIL Service Transition*) A pre-authorized change that is low risk, relatively common and follows a procedure or work instruction – for example, a password reset or provision of standard equipment to a new employee. Requests for change are not required to implement a standard change, and they are logged and tracked using a different mechanism, such as a service request.

storage management

(*ITIL Service Operation*) The process responsible for managing the storage and maintenance of data throughout its lifecycle.

super user

(*ITIL Service Operation*) A user who helps other users, and assists in communication with the service desk or other parts of the IT service provider. Super users are often experts in the business processes supported by an IT service and will provide support for minor incidents and training.

supplier

(*ITIL Service Design*) (*ITIL Service Strategy*) A third party responsible for supplying goods or services that are required to deliver IT services. Examples of suppliers include commodity hardware and software vendors, network and telecom providers, and outsourcing organizations.

support group

(*ITIL Service Operation*) A group of people with technical skills. Support groups provide the technical support needed by all of the IT service management processes.

support hours

(*ITIL Service Design*) (*ITIL Service Operation*) The times or hours when support is available to the users. Typically these are the hours when the service desk is available. Support hours should be defined in a service level agreement, and may be different from service hours. For example, service hours may be 24 hours a day, but the support hours may be 07:00 to 19:00.

supporting service

(*ITIL Service Design*) An IT service that is not directly used by the business, but is required by the IT service provider to deliver customer-facing services (for example, a directory service or a backup service). Supporting services may also include IT services only used by the IT service provider. All live supporting services, including those available for deployment, are recorded in the service catalogue along with information about their relationships to customer-facing services and other CIs.

technical observation

(*ITIL Continual Service Improvement*) (*ITIL Service Operation*) A technique used in service improvement, problem investigation and availability management. Technical support staff meet to monitor the behaviour and performance of an IT service and make recommendations for improvement.

third-line support

(*ITIL Service Operation*) The third level in a hierarchy of support groups involved in the resolution of incidents and investigation of problems. Each level contains more specialist skills, or is allocated more time or other resources.

threshold

The value of a metric that should cause an alert to be generated or management action to be taken. For example, 'Priority 1 incident not solved within four hours', 'More than five soft disk errors in an hour', or 'More than 10 failed changes in a month'.

urgency

(*ITIL Service Design*) (*ITIL Service Transition*) A measure of how long it will be until an incident, problem or change has a significant impact on the business. For example, a high-impact incident may have low urgency if the impact will not affect the business until the end of the financial year. Impact and urgency are used to assign priority.

user

A person who uses the IT service on a day-to-day basis. Users are distinct from customers, as some customers do not use the IT service directly.

workaround

(*ITIL Service Operation*) Reducing or eliminating the impact of an incident or problem for which a full resolution is not yet available – for example, by restarting a failed configuration item. Workarounds for problems are documented in known error records. Workarounds for incidents that do not have associated problem records are documented in the incident record.